Retrieving service laterally

Face-

Volleyball game theory and drills

Two-h

Two-hand pass with lateral fall

VOLLEYBALL GAME THEORY AND DRILLS

Effective training and strategies

Written by **Berthold Fröhner, PhD**

Edited by **Tiit T. Romet, PhD**
Peter Klavora, PhD
School of Physical and Health Education
University of Toronto

Sport Books Publisher Toronto

Translation by Linda Paul

Canadian Cataloguing in Publication Data

Fröhner, Bernthold
  Volleyball: game theory and drills

1st Canadian ed.
Translation of: Spiele für das Volleyballtraining.
ISBN 0-920905-36-6

1. Volleyball - Training. I. Romet, T. T. (Tiit T.).
II. Title

GV1015.5.T73F7613 1990 796.32'5 C89-094511-X

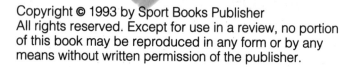

Distribution in Canada and worldwide by
Sport Books Publisher
278 Robert Street
Toronto, Ontario M5S 2K8

Printed in the United States

Contents

6

How to Use this Book

The objective of this book is to help players and coaches organize technique and tactics training in interesting and diverse ways. The book offers readers a basis in theory combined with the opportunity to put this theory into practice. It enables them to organize *volleyball training based on actual game conditions* through a selection of suitable drills and games that do not entail major written preparation.

1. First, turn to the table fo contents to give yourself a general picture of the organization of the book.
2. Then read Chapter 1. It provides the basic information necessary for a methodical approach to technique and tactics training and for the selection of drills. The use of the term play for volleyball training to describe the content of drills stresses the objective of this book. These types of drills are closely oriented towards these motor and mental demands made on players during the game. Players acquire and practise these volleyball-specific abilities and skills in drills modelled from the game itself, thereby ensuring from the outset their capacity for adapting to future situations and demands.
3. The most significant fundamentals in training methodology are presented in Chapter 2. Proceed directly from this section to preparing the material for your practice sessions.
4. Use the pictorial appendix, the illustrations of the movements on the front and back jacket, as well as the description of the essential points of technique to ensure that you and the players can visualize the motions correctly.
5. Familiarize yourself with the general sequence of elements to be learned and then concentrate on learning each of the elements in the game. Working through the description of the game elements, observations on the learning process, and training hints will enable you to organize training more effectively.
6. It is especially important to consider Sections 2.1, 2.2, 2.3 as a whole and to combine them with the tactical rules on how to use the game elements effectively (Sections 3.1.4, 3.2.4, etc.). Observing the

proposed recommendations will help you to set the objectives and tasks in your training program. Use the tactical rules to set clear practice and game tasks and teach these to your players as basic tactical knowledge.

7. Set up practice and game related drills that correspond to the training levels of your group. Throughout the book you will find cross-references, making the location of the individual drills easier.

8. The drills are based on actual game elements familiar to players in volleyball and are informatively presented and described.

9. Use the following procedure for reading the drills:
   - unfold the book jacket.
   - the legend includes the figures, arrows (indicating running and moving), as well as other symbols that form the basis for a stylized drill description. Players are sometimes identified by letters for easier reference in the text. Numbers show the path of the ball. A brief verbal description on the diagrams indicates the organizational principle used.
   - read the caption underneath the illustration and follow the sequence in the drill with the aid of the symbols used and the path of the ball, which is numbered. The information contained in the captions can be used as guide for organizing practice. Be creative with the drills, tailoring them to the needs of your particular group.
   - remember that the drill is merely a framework. Its effectiveness in the training process is determined above all by your degree of success in following the instructions for organizing practice as closely to game conditions as possible (Chapter 2.5), the tactical rules, and the particular aspects of each stage of play (Chapter 1.5)
   - note of the drill numbers when you are preparing for training. Use the book to explain elements in the drills in the practice session itself and to provide players with a basis in game's theory.

1 The Game of Volleyball

1.1 Game Description

Volleyball, an extremely popular team sport, belongs to a group of receiving sports played on teams. Two teams stand on opposite sides of a court divided into two equal parts by a net. The standard court dimensions (9m X 18m), net height (2.24m or 2.43m), and the number of players ("6 on 6") may be geared towards actual player development or to meet the needs of particular groups. The game is played to win points, sets, and finally, the match. There is no time limit. Without coming into direct physical contact with the opposing team, each side tries to put the ball into the opponents' court in such a manner that it falls to the floor or cannot be returned over the net. The ball may be played a maximum of three times on each team before it must be played into the opponents' court. Faults result in points being awarded or a change in service. The rotation of players clockwise to the next position when they have regained the service is essential; it ensures that each player on a team plays all positions on the floor and prevents specialization in any one floor position in offence and defence.

Fifteen points with a two point margin are necessary to win the set. To win the match a team must win 3 sets. Since only the team serving can score points, playing the game is influenced by two fundamental aspects of the game:

1. Retaining service = having the initiative = offensive playing style, willing to take risks with the aim of scoring more points.
2. Losing service to opposing team = loss of initiative = faults result in loss of points; game is played according to the principle "certainty before risk taking".

We shall refer to these aspects as Complex I and Complex II in volleyball. They are important in determining the ultimate objective of all the players of a team. Each team tries to win points and prevent the other team from doing so and thus achieve the final victory. The rules of the game, its breakdown into specific components and the conditions given for completing these components (game rules, playing area) restrict the players' freedom of movement and at the same time establish fundamental interrelationships in their team play (see Section 1.2.).

Each player is in a constantly changing relationship with teammates, opponents, playing area, and the ball. The fundamental elements of volleyball (ball may be played only three times, no catching, throwing, carrying the ball—relying on the judgement of the referee—rotational order, etc.) require a great deal of versatility during play and above all an exact "feeling" for the ball. Players must take an active part both mentally and physically in the game. The game rules prevent zealous play (no consecutive touches by the same player), ensuring that success in the game is determined largely by team play (co-operation) and how it is organized (communication = aural and visual exchange of information). These aspects of team play among players should be integrated with opponents' behaviour. The opponents' intentions must be identified soon enough to enable players to act correctly, individually and collectively. It is these relationships that give the game of volleyball its characteristic "structure."

1.2   The Play Structure

The major characteristic of volleyball is the integration of a quick succession of different and rapidly changing game situations.

Although the game is very complex and may at times appear confusing to the observer, the sequence of events in the game is not random but is to a large extent governed by the rules of the game.

Seen from the outside, specific *game phases* (e.g., passing serve, setting - attacking or blocking - defence on court - digging - counterattack) occur repeatedly at regular intervals. These game phases are always the same or a least similar. We notice, however, that during different game phases different responsibilities dominate, confronting players and the team as a whole with continually changing tasks. Players cope with these conditions in various ways by using highly specific, more-or-less conscious actions or *game plays*. These games plays demand accurate *decision making*. Decision making is possible only when information has been received and processed. Early identification and assessment of a situation, mental anticipation, evaluation of options, and selection of the most appropriate solution are key elements in volleyball. Players therefore must work just as conscientiously at planning and decision making as at the quality of their motor performance. Changing or following the tactical game plan of the coach should also be considered part of this process.

- As a result of the quickly changing game situations all game plays are compressed into a narrow time frame. Together, with the wide range of information available during the course of play and the expectation of performance, *high levels of concentration* are necessary and must be maintained over an extended period of time (game time), despite psychological stresses and physical strain.
- The variability of game situations and stages in play requires an *extensive repertory of motor skills.* Putting a specific planned action into play can be done only within this framework, i.e., players can only make decisions for which corresponding motor skills exist. Although a good mastery of the techniques involved is of course important for the successful outcome of the game, the accuracy of the decision-making process based on the situation is of prime importance during the game.
- Players' actions are largely determined by actions of their opponents. The difficult co-ordination of movement combinations, the maximum precision required during execution, and the limited amount of time for playing the ball also become important factors. Particular emphasis should, however, be placed on a relatively large freedom for movement when executing sequences of movements. There are almost always several possible motor/technical solutions for a game situation. We also therefore speak of *decision-making actions.*
- Players must execute motor movements of varying levels of difficulty. These movements, whether with or without the ball, do not constitute an end in themselves, but rather aid in fulfilling a wide variety of game tasks with the objective of winning the game. In other words, players act purposefully, using *effective tactics* within the framework mentioned earlier and within the individual and game situations that occur. The observable physical activity is only the final part of a complex action, in which motor skill and physical capabilities dominate.
- *The complex structure of game activity* is expressed in the interaction between motor skills, as well as tactical (individual and team), psychological, and fitness factors. Describing the game activity only in terms of technique and tactics is therefore incorrect. All of the components mentioned are related to each other and weaknesses may only be compensated for to a limited extent through individual performance. As the quality of team performance increases, development of individual skills alone can not improve the overall team quality.
- In addition to studying and working, playing is one of our main forms of activity. Fulfilling performance demands during the game, in particular *the quality of* decision-making *processes* (conscious determination of action goals and the methods necessary for their realization) is determined, as in other forms of activity, to a great extent by both *motiva-*

tional as well as by *emotional factors.*

1.3   Game Elements, Game Plays, Game Situations, and Game Phases

When we consider the typical features of playing activity we become aware that players' actions or *game plays* are not simply responses to random external influences, but deliberate actions for achieving pre-determined objectives. Psychological and motor processes are very important to completing game plays, even those that do not always involve playing with the ball.

We shall give two possible definitions of this important term:

1. Game plays are more or less complex effective combinations of different psychological and motor processes essential for solving a particular game task.
2. A game play is the effective tactical conduct for optimum continuation of the game by a player in a specific situation, in which numerous stimuli are present.

The following *game elements* typically occur during the game: service, passing of serve, setting, attack, block, defence, and free ball passing. They are the main components of the game, but by themselves they do not make "play" possible beacause they constitute merely specific combinations of movements without taking into account the psychological aspect involved. Although at this point we do not want to subdivide the game elements into part movements, we would like to point out that during the progression of play three distinct stages are present:

1. perception and analysis of the game situation (gathering information and information-receiving);
2. mental processing of the situation and coming to an accurate decision (information-processing); and
3. translating the solution of the play situation into motor action with the pre-planned "programme of movement."

They are closely associated with three observable stages in actual movement:

- preparatory stage (ready position, movement towards ball);
- main stage (play position, body position immediately before and after

play with ball, action with ball); and
- final stage (body position after action with ball, follow-through, moving to next game play).

As we shall see later, paying attention to these phases does play a vital role in the progression of play actions.

The fact that a team may play a ball up to three times entails a quick change in attack and defence as a regular feature of the play. Together with inbuilt preparatory phases or ready phases (formation for receiving serve, organizing attack and block cover, etc.) there are fluid transitions in allocating play elements to attack and defence.

Although the classification of many game elements (e.g., serve, attack setup) into attack or defence is obvious, it is not so easy to classify several others (e.g., as the first play following the opponents' serve). Some game elements are on the one hand, defensive in nature, but if performed accurately, have a decisive and direct influence on how the next attack is carried out (see mandatory actions).

The purposeful use of game elements, including all their variations under different conditions, to fulfil game tasks results *in game plays*. We shall refer to the complex of conditions for combining the game elements as the *game situation*. These conditions are the result of the position and action of teammates and opponents as well as the position or movement of the ball.

The most significant game elements are presented in Diagram 1. These stand out as prominent aspects of the game, but at the same time they can undergo rapid change and might therefore be subdivided even further. From the player's viewpoint it is primarily important to react to the continually changing game situations by means of their individual play actions without any direct co-operation from other players.

An exact analysis of the game reveals, however, that the game elements or situations are linked together by a characteristic form that reoccurs in the same or at least a similar manner (e.g., retrieving serve-setting - attack). Each game play is almost always a part of a sequence or chain of actions. We refer to these typical motor sequences as *game phases* (see Chapter 1.5).

Players and teammates must ensure the successful flow of the game and complete each sequence of actions. Tactical action is optimum when they fulfil each of the component tasks, taking into consideration the ultimate objective.

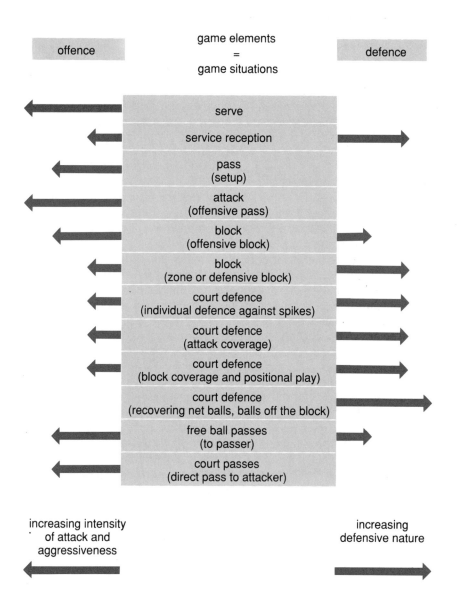

Diagram 1 A summary chart showing game elements and their nature.

1.4   How a Game Play is Made

Often older players with extensive competitive experience can compensate for the advantages in physical ability of younger players by superior technique and tactics. They simply have a better overall perspective and greater insight into the game. They are able to see the relationships more clearly, to select and process the most important information from the game, compare it with previous experience, and come up with the correct solution for the situation, often in a short period of time.

We have previously explained that play activity always requires attention to the "game situation—game action" interrelationship. The game task, i.e., the motor objective and conditions for completing the action, is always a product of the game situation. This explains why, for example, a player cannot concentrate exclusively on motor performance and "rehearse" it completely mentally beforehand like a gymnast. Players must be able to react to other actions already in progress besides their own, adapt to the situation, while at the same time remaining capable of anticipating the outcome of their actions and establishing workable motor patterns to complete the phase. For this they must use their store of tactical knowledge, and experience dealing with a wide variety of previous play situations.

The advantage that seasoned players have is that they have resolved many similar situations and can automatically retrieve a solution from memory. Yet, after what has been said above, it seems reasonable not to rely solely upon experience gained in competition over many years to become a good player, but rather to use training and practice sessions to shorten the path towards this goal. This can be achieved by teaching players drills related closely to game situations and game phases.

We should not concentrate exclusively on training the motor skill aspects of game plays and separate them from actual game conditions. By teaching the specific movements in the early stages of training with a view to applying them under specific conditions later, and by organizing the drills so that they reflect a repeated solution to equal or similar situations, we insert an essential (effective) stage between technique training and games training. The result is an intensified training process and, as experience shows, this has a major effect on improving the learning process.

Six steps form the basis of this learning process, and players must go through them when completing a play in volleyball or in any other sport. We shall attempt to describe them in the following.

Step one: Setting an objective

Athletes must be given a game goal or be able to set it themselves. The better they are able to relate to the goal or elements of that goal, the more likely they will go about solving the task. This step can be accomplished with increased success if both practice and game goals are similar (see Chapter 2.5.).

Step two: Orientation

Players must identify a particular game condition and the various possibilities for action quickly. It is ideal, of course, when players can recall from memory the appropriate responses. If this recall process takes too long, players will be swamped by the action of the game, making execution of the appropriate motor skill impossible. To acquire the ability to identify and respond correctly to these situations, they must be placed in game situations or actions during practice that resemble those they will face in a future match.

Step three: Planning

Players should not attempt motor execution without thought. They must remove themselves from the actual situation and mentally plan the appropriate response. They should plan their motor skill response from the different possibilities available and select the most appropriate one. This process, which contains the essential elements of the planned action and intended result, is decisive in the whole learning process, and must become the motor skill programme that guides the motor behaviour and at the same time monitors it.

Step four: Making a decision

An important phase has been reached when players recognize that there are many different ways to achieve a goal. They must choose from the options available, determine the objective, and decide upon a specific motor skill. Only when they have made this decision is the way finally clear for them to begin the action. Practice will show whether the action chosen is the right one.

A thorough knowledge of the game is essential to making the correct decision. It can be acquired through practice (when resolving game situations), but it can also be gained through theoretical knowledge and instruction.

Step five: Execution

The fifth step is the action itself, its motor performance. Those who have not completed the preceding steps carefully will stumble at this point. Players must transfer what they have practised mentally into actual motor performance. They will not always be completely successful. However, even when players have successfully managed this transfer, it is important that they learn how to analyze the actual motor execution, i.e., the end motor product: this produces positive results that can be stored in memory for future decision-making.

Step six: Evaluation and feedback

The mental process developed during stage three, which contains both the motor objective and the plan for its execution, remains intact even after the immediate execution of the motor skill. The effectiveness of that process can be checked easily and information received through the sensory organs during motor performance evaluated.

The comparison between required or intended versus actual results during and following motor activity (in-course and final check) determines the accuracy of the performance; it calls upon players to correct any discrepancies immediately and to prevent them from recurring. This controlled ability is an expression of conscious learning. Coaches must support it by teaching the relevant facts and also by correcting their students.

These six steps cannot be separated clearly from one another. They are interrelated and occur together during play. They constitute a theoretical model that should heighten understanding of the psychological and motor processes that occur in the interplay between game situation and game play.

1.5   Typical Game Phases in Volleyball

If we disregard a few that are resolved in a relatively isolated manner (i.e., serve), almost all game situations are found in the 10 principal game phases outlined in Diagram 3. These game phases are typical and are interrelated in different ways. The differences between them becomes apparent in the different combination of defensive plays (mandatory or key movements, as they are known), variations in offensive formation, and in offensive conclusion.

As well as working out characteristic motor sequences it is possible to distinguish, on the basis of observation and analysis, a pattern of purposeful tactical behaviour for each play phase on which the player may orient himself.

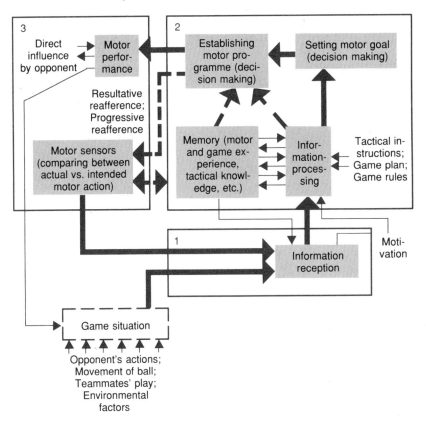

Diagram 2   A simplified model of a game play showing relationship and mutual interdependencies among game situations and play sections.

There are always several possible solutions for the same game phase. Players must always conform their actions to the game phase taking place and decide which actions can be successfully completed from their repertory of movements and tactics. This requires careful tactical preparation. Teaching players about the motor correlations in volleyball enables them to process the information "bombarding" them during a game and helps them make the best possible decision to resolve the game situation (as a part of the game phase). We have no ready-made formulas for this process; players are instead given drills to improve decision making both individually and as a team. This places individual tactics associated with individual action (game situation) into a broader context, which all players involved in each of the game phases can use as a reference, regardless at which point in the phase they complete their individual task. An example below will illustrate this notion.

Let us consider Game Phase 3 (easy ball from opponent - pass - attack from combination passes). The defensive player must decide whether a volley or bump pass can be made. An individual decision must be made, a decision bound by the requirement for maximum accuracy in motor performance and made with the knowledge that the passes are essential for the setup that follows. The attackers also use a tactical framework associated with the successful resolution of this game phase and ready themselves to make special passes for the purposes of executing the actual offensive play with effective individual tactics. In this way all players may use this entire tactical framework as a guide, doing their specific share to ensure success in the game phase and so becoming aware of the correspondence between plays in the game.

	1	2	3	4	5	6	7	8	9	10
Defence										
Service receive	●	●				●				
Court pass			●							
Block (no contact with ball)/defence					●		●			
Block (with ball contact)/defence								●		
Court defence (coverage)			●							
Development of play										
Specific passes	●		●	●	●			●		
High parallel passes	●	●	●	●				●		
High diagonal passes					●		●	●	●	
Attack										
Spike from attack sets	●		●	●	●			●		
Spike from high parallel passes		●	●	●	●			●		
Spike from high diagonal passes					●		●	●	●	
Balls from opponent									●	
Attack from backcourt										●

Diagram 3   Typical game phases.

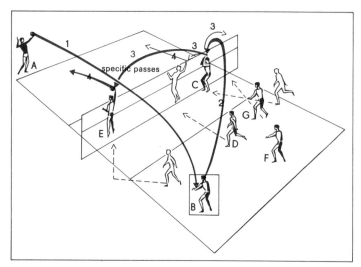

Game Phase 1:
Service Reception – Set Pass (Attack Sets) – Attack

The first game phase is characterized by the sequence "bumping - attack sets - spike." By attack sets is meant short passes at position 3, long flat passes to position 4, metre balls, cross variations and other forms for setting, all of which are used to initiate offensive combinations. Playing this first phase successfully is crucial in scoring side outs and achieving an effective overall attack. Receiving accuracy is critical for bringing about this phase; its effective solution depends in turn on the concerted efforts of the ball-passing player and the attack formation of attackers. All three attackers take part in the offence. Their crucial positioning to divert the block (especially at position 3) and various passing tactics aid considerably in the successful completion of the spike. This phase is present about 20% (maximum 40%) of the time in all game phases.

In the diagram, player A hits the serve to player B, who bumps the ball directly to passer C (setter), therefore creating phase one. Reception accuracy is the key to the success of this phase. For this reason, we refer to all initiatory plays as "key" plays or mandatory plays. Setter C makes a long flat pass to attacker E. The latter spikes the ball, and, at the same time, players G and D are in attack formation. By co-ordinating their actions it is possible for the setter to choose different variations when preparing for the attack thus making it difficult for the opponents' block to act.

The following is a summary of rules for successful play in Game

Phase 1:

1. Try to achieve maximum accuracy when bumping the serve. It is crucial for bringing about the first game phase.
2. By using an active attack formation (especially at position 3), the attackers divert the attention of the opposing team's block. This together with fake passes creates favourable conditions for an attack.
3. Attack powerfully and without compromise. "Attack—turn and hit the ball together with individual play" proves to be most effective.
4. The phase is played successfully when there is good co-ordination between setter and attacker principally in standard combinations.

Remember!
- Maximum reception accuracy is critical.
- Divert the attention of the block by active attack formation.
- Emphasis should be on hard spike.
- Passes should be concealed.
- Team play between setter and attackers is essential.

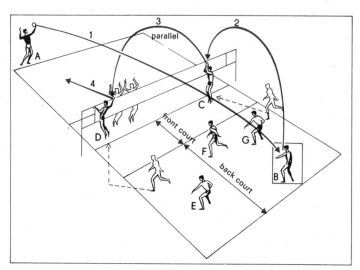

Game Phase 2:
Service Reception – Set Pass – Attack (High Passes)

The second game phase also belongs to those present during opponents' serve. It is characterized by the sequence "bumping - high parallel
passes - spike." With a high set the phase is deliberately initiated and
provides an alternative to the quick attack combination. Whereas this
phase is present in competitive volleyball between 10 and 20% of the time
in all the phases, completing this phase successfully, generally speaking,
has a major role in the game (in connection with attack formation using
frontcourt passer).

Successful play of this phase is determined primarily by the actions
of each attacker when spiking past a block that is well formed.

In view of the better chances for a successful attack in Game Phase
1, it is important to reduce the share of Game Phase 2 in favour of special,
though initially simple attack combinations. This requires high precision
and stability when receiving the serve as a key action for the occurrence
of the two game phases.

In the diagram, player A bats the service to player B, who bumps the
ball to frontcourt. Passer C volleys high parallel pass to attacker D. Player
D varies attack on block formation.

Basic concepts to remember during Game Phase 2 combinations
are:

1. Try to bump difficult serves accurately to frontcourt. While in many cases maximum accuracy is essential for special offensive combinations (phase 1), bumping is done only with a certain amount of risk; therefore it is better to ensure favourable conditions for high setup of the ball.

2. Play safe, high passes as safe alternatives to specific combination passes.
3. Play to attackers at outside positions as much as possible (power hitters).
4. Only use off speed and tips when they can be justified tactically, but not as awkward solutions or "alibi attacks."
5. Attack vigorously and without compromise. Spikes with change of direction and hitting against the block are especially effective.
6. Jump to maximum height and hit at the highest point with arm extended.

Remember!

- Consistency when bumping is more important than maximum accuracy.
- Play safe, high passes.
- Play to outside positions 2 and 4.
- Use off speeds and tips - tactical shots.
- Variable and fierce attack; hitting against the block.
- Aim for maximum height before contacting the ball.

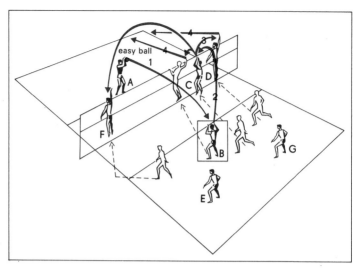

Game Phase 3:
Easy Ball from Opponent — Court Pass — Set Pass — Attack

As a result of good offensive play an opposing team can often only play the ball back in a haphazard manner. This gives the typical sequence for Game Phase 3 "court pass after receiving an easy ball from opponent - high and attack passes - spike."

The development of this stage is clear: when court passes are accurate, the attack can be completed quickly and, using a high percentage of special offensive combinations (70% and more for top-league teams), with an element of surprise. In addition to good court passes, smooth team play between the setter and attackers is also important in the success of this stage. If a team plans to use many combinations in the game, it must consistently move into the attack formation in this phase. However, beginners must concentrate on accurate execution of the key element, the "court pass," without which they can seldom complete a specific offensive combination. Careful compliance with this rule is an important step towards systematic but fluid play and should be seen as the chief criterion the first time this game phase is initiated.

In the diagram, the opponent passes an easy ball to player B. Setter C has recognized the progression in the phase and prepares for pass. Player B makes an accurate court pass. All three attackers ready themselves for attack; player B is particularly important in attacking quickly to freeze the middle blocker.

Passer C selects his attackers, using as guides the conduct of opposing block and "conceals" his passes as much as possible. Attacker makes a powerful spike.

In summary, we have once again a few points of reference for correct completion of this phase:

1. Ensure from the beginning that court passes are as accurate as possible – the key for playing this phase successfully.
2. The setter who seizes the right moment and active formation (quick transition) by attackers makes good team play possible and therefore contributes to effective tactical offence.
3. Diverting the attention of the middle blocker and concealing passes encumber the opponents' blocking play.
4. With increased skill use rapid and surprising offensive variations. Game Phase 3 is especially appropriate for this.
5. Attack hard and without compromise as in Game Phase 1.

Remember!

- Maximum accuracy of court pass is crucial.
- The passer should immediately prepare himself for the set-up.
- The block's attention should be diverted by attackers getting ready to play the ball.
- Try to use increasing number of specific offensive combinations.
- Be hard and uncompromising when completing attack.

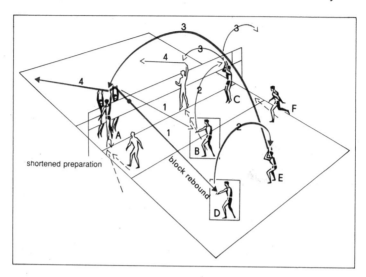

shortened preparation

block rebound

Game Phase 4:
Block Rebound – Court Attack/Court Pass – Set Pass – Attack

A particular type of transition between "court defence - counter-attack" occurs when the spike rebounds immediately from the block back into the team's own half of the court. Defensive players must try to bump the rebounds from the block, which are often unpredictable, allowing an attack once again. The variable aspect of this phase and the abrupt change to new motor sequences without any time for preparation requires good organization in the attack coverage (coverage of own attackers, close to the block and farther from the block). Depending upon the difficulty of playing the blocked ball, players can choose between a normal attack formation (Game Phase 2) and the use of specific passes to accelerate play (Game Phase 3). Shifting the attack to another net position is usually an effective tactic.

In the diagram, player A spikes the ball into the closed two-player block. The ball rebounds from block; player D bumps it to player E. Player A resumes attack formation once more, receives the diagonal pass from player F and spikes past the block. Another possible solution is for player C to receive the bump directly from B or D. Attackers B and F assume attack formation and a quick pass is made to one of them.

Playing this phase successfully requires particular attention to several points:

1. Covering the attack requires planned and organized action. Quick transition between coverage play and renewed attack formation should be made.
2. Organized positioning is essential for attack coverage and provides good team play in both short- and long-distance coverage. Never assume that the attacker will be successful.
3. Always be alert and mobile on the court, ready for possible coverage play. Never assume that the attacker will score points no matter what you do.
4. When resuming attack formation execute simply and safely; and whenever possible attack from the outside positions.
5. An established system avoids restlessness among players and aimless play. Only use specific attack combinations when the phase will allow for good team play between passer and attackers.
6. Always be prepared to play under difficult conditions (e.g., short preparation for attack), and be prepared for the worse-case scenario and increased concentration and aggressive play.

Remember!

- Adapt quickly to the subsequent action.
- Cover in a planned and orderly fashion.
- Be alert and mobile on the court – it is basis for quick reaction.
- Choose normal attack formation at outside positions 2 and 4.
- Do not use specific offensive combinations indiscriminately.
- Practise often under difficult conditions.

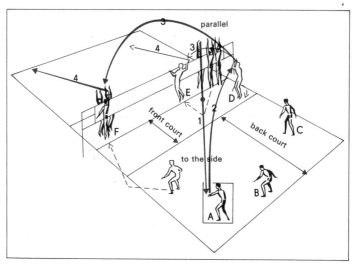

Game Phase 5:
No Block Contact – Dig – Set-up (Parallel) – Attack

Several game phases are characterized by the transition "court defence-counter attack." They occur following the team's own serve or during continuation of play if Game Phases 1, 2, and 6 were neither a complete success nor a complete failure. These phases are imbedded in the course of play, occur irregularly, and assume different forms. Playing them successfully means that greater demands are made on players than in Game Phases 1, 2, and 6, which occur immediately after opponents' serve or easy ball and which are relatively clear and predictable.

The sequence "opponents' spike without block contact - bump to frontcourt - high and specific passes - spike" is typical of Game Phase 5. With good team play between the blockers and defensive players, the ball is bumped to the attack zone, making offensive play possible from high, specific passes. Aggressive play by blockers and defensive players as well as the rapid transition to attack are physically demanding, yet the quality of action must not be allowed to diminish. This phase requires creative solutions: normal, safe play formation, instead of complicated special offensive combinations, is recommended.

In the diagram, opponent G at position 4 spikes the ball past block. Player A bumps the ball directly to passer D, who plays a high parallel pass to position 4. Attacker F spikes down the line. Players A, B and C cover. As a variation, a quick set is made to player E at position 3.

The following basic rules should be observed:

1. Try to close the block as the basis of successful court defence.
2. Tempo and variety of play often call for rapid change from block/bump to return spike or counter attack.
3. Aggressive play, especially at position 3 (middle blocker), is the basis for effective use of specific offensive combinations.
4. Attack aggressively and in different ways, even under difficult conditions (short preparation). Although simple, high ball offence is dominant, take advantage of specific combinations.
5. Constant participation, even without the ball, total involvement, and maximum concentration are the basic requirements for successful play during rapid play sequence.

Remember!

- Closed block is the basis for success in court defence.
- Quick change from block/court defence to attack is necessary.
- Aggressive play, especially at position 3, for attack combinations is important.
- Great demands on quality of motor action are made under physical strain.
- Attack forcefully, using mostly simple, well learned combinations.
- Aggressive play is a fundamental condition of successful play.

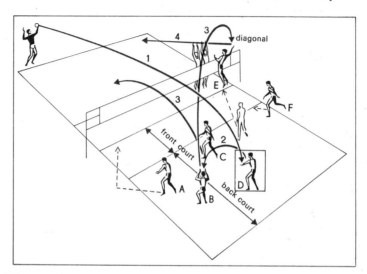

Game Phase 6:
Receiving Serve – Set-up (from Back Court) – Attack

Game Phase 6 marks the end of phases that occur after opponents' serve. Since the ball is bumped inaccurately, the spike is made from high, often diagonal, passes from the backcourt. The success of this phase depends upon accuracy of the high passes and upon attackers' technique and tactics. Since there is no element of surprise in this play, the attacker must almost always be prepared for a two-player block. A high frequency of blocked spikes rebounding back into court requires attentive attack coverage. This is often the case 5% to 10% of the time. If it occurs too frequently (on account of poor serve receive), offensive success will be hampered considerably.

In the diagram, player G serves to player D. Back-row setter F assumes normal setting position; ball is bumped, however, indirectly to player B in the backcourt. The latter makes a high diagonal pass to attacker E or A, who prepares for the attack at an outside position. One of them spikes the ball.

In spite of reduced chances for success in this phase, it is important to take note of the following:

1. Improve bumping of the ball, thereby preventing frequent occurrence of this game phase.
2. Play high passes in front of attacker and not too close to the net. Ensure that attackers can also master the high pass from the

backcourt.
3. Stage attack at outside positions 2 and particularly 4; this is the most effective strategy.
4. Jump to maximum height for a spike. Negotiate the block actively. Smash with changing direction and keep the number of lobs and feints/tips to a minimum.
5. As a rule, the well-formed two-player block forces players covering an attack to be constantly prepared.

Remember!
- Prevent repeated occurrence of this game phase with accurate serve reception.
- Maintain maximum setup accuracy.
- In general, stage attacks at outside positions.
- Negotiate the block actively.
- Success depends on the individual ability of attackers.
- Concentrate on readiness for attack coverage.

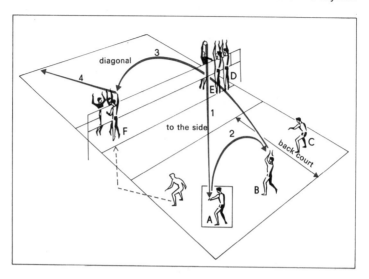

Game Phase 7:
Without Block Contact – Court Defence – Set-up (from Back Court) – Attack

In this phase, as in Game Phase 5, the block does not make contact with or deflect the opponents' spikes. Following inaccurate court defence into the back court, attack is launched from high diagonal passes. The diminished accuracy of the bump pass must be offset by more vigorous setting and aggressive spiking of the ball.

Once again, the successful solution of this phase rests upon the rapid transition from block/court defence to counter-attack. Since the attack is frequently blocked when spiking from high diagonal passes, alert attack coverage is required. As in Game Phase 5, a spike is often made after physically strenuous plays.

In the diagram, player G hits the ball past the block formation by players D and E to player A. The latter then bumps the ball indirectly, forcing player B to play a high diagonal pass to position 4. When F spikes the ball, players A, B, and C ensure attack coverage.

As in Game Phase 5, be prepared for rapid and unpredictable play. The rapid sequence in blocking, bumping, and spiking causes great physical demands. However, the quality of action must not suffer; use simple tactics by moving attack to outside positions, especially position 4.

Remember!
- Quick change from block/defence to attack is important.
- Great demands are made on quality of action under physical strain.
- Prefer attack from outside positions.
- Attack offensively despite difficult conditions.
- Pay special attention to attack coverage.

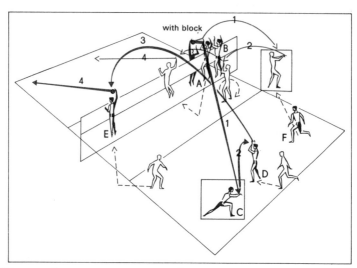

Game Phase 8:
Hitting the Block – Court Defence/Court Pass – Set Pass – Attack

A typical feature of this game phase is the bumping of opponents' spikes which have been weakened or deflected clearly by a block. This basic phase therefore contains many unpredictable variations during defence and the transition to offense that place great demands on perception, analysis, and creative playing of this game phase. Depending upon the result of the block, the offensive movement or transition is begun from various defensive plays, ranging from passes on court to the rapid defence of difficult block rebounds. Depending upon bumping accuracy, high sets are most often made, although quick offensive combinations are also used. Aggressive blocking and concentration when digging "deactivate" the opponents' attack and allow your players to gain control of the game. The setter has a great deal of responsibility and must spot quickly an opportunity for using special offensive combinations, moving swiftly to the setting position by the net, and initiating the attack with specific passes.

The diagram shows a spike by player G, which is clearly thwarted by the block formed by players A and B into the playing area of player C. This last player bumps the ball high to backcourt; player D runs for the ball and makes a high pass to attacker E.

In one of the many variations, the ball bounces into defensive area of player F, who plays the ball successfully, and keeps it in play. Players A and B break away quickly from the block. Player B plays the ball quickly to player A, who has prepared himself for attacking quickly. Here are a few suggestions for effective play:

1. Try to block effectively. This increases the chances for success in defending, leading to a counter-attack.
2. Bumping deflected spikes requires enormous concentration for accurate execution, especially for careful bumps to the setter.
3. Take advantage of opportunities for special offensive combinations. Keep in mind the setter's responsibility as the central figure in this play formation.
4. The variable course of this phase places great demands on the ability to react swiftly, to differentiate intelligently, and to change or adapt to other plays.

Remember!

- Be aggressive during blocking and court defense - it is the basis for successful counter attacks.
- Bump accurately.
- An active back-row setter creates increased attack possibilities.
- Make planned use of specific offensive combinations.
- Great demands are made on a team's co-ordination.

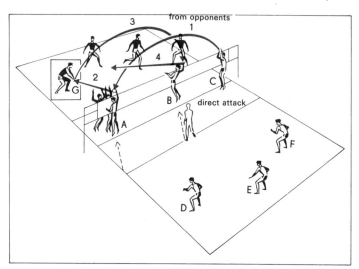

Game Phase 9:
Attack with Balls Coming from the Opponent

The typical game phases in volleyball are completed by two special cases, which are rather rare. In this game phase, the spike is made directly off balls coming back from the opposing team.

This can occur following your own team's attack or a poor play of their own (bumping, defence on court, overset), where the ball is practically over the top of the net. Careful observation of the game and aggressive play by those without the ball make for successful attacks, often with short preparation time. Playing the phase successfully with consistently powerful spikes has an important psychological effect. Its rare occurrence—approximately every 30th series of plays or phases—means that it is imperative to play this game phase successfully.

In the diagram, player C sets a low ball to position 4. Player A spikes the ball past the block to player G, who can only bump the ball when close to net. Player B seizes opportunity for a direct spike and immediately returns the "ball from the opponent" as a powerful spike.

Here, once again, are a few rules for effective play:

1. Always take an active part in play, so that you can follow the progression of the phase early on and can prepare for the attack.
2. Make use of the significant psychological effect associated with the successful and consistent attacks of "balls from the opponent."
3. Despite favourable conditions do not try to "overkill." Remember the

danger of the smash trap, the poor observation of the flight of the ball and then an often too late hit resulting in a spike into the net. At all costs, do not pull it down towards you in an attempt to hit it hard.

4. If the chances for making a direct spike are restricted by shortened preparation time, it is then better to resort to the normal offensive pattern.

Remember!

- Attentive observation of play is important.
- Make use of psychological effect of successful spike.
- Do not try to "overkill" the attack; consider using a normal offensive formation as well.
- Prepare for an attack with shorter preparation time.

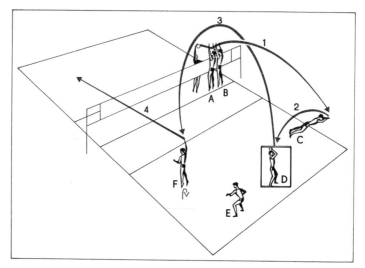

Game Phase 10:
Attack from Backcourt

Game Phase 10 completes the typical phases in volleyball. Its character-istics will be examined from two angles. On one hand, "attacks (spikes) from backcourt" are carried out after faults in preceding plays. Players attempt, with justifiable risk, to make an attack into that opponents' court. On the other hand, in modern volleyball we increasingly find a deliberate transfer of the attack into backcourt (behind the attack line). Two sequences are characteristic of the newly developed offensive tactics: the accurate playing of high passes into the backcourt instead of diagonal passes to positions 2 and 4; and the deceptive introduction of special offensive combinations at positions 2/3, with the attack (spike) completed using passes at half the normal height behind the attack line or simple high setting to a tall attacker in the backcourt.

In the diagram, we see the first variation of this phase. Spike by player G rebounds from block into far backcourt. With considerable effort player C makes save. Player D succeeds only, however, in making a high pass to backcourt, which player F then uses for a spike.

The following rules should be observed for effective play:

1. Despite limited possibilities, attack with justifiable risk or aggression, but ensure that your own team has serve.
2. Hit the balls diagonally into opponents' court, thus increasing the chances for the power spikes to hit the court.

3. The deliberate transfer of the attack to the backcourt is suitable only for experienced players who possess good offensive techniques and who are physically able to meet these demands.

Remember!

- With justifiable risk, an offensive attack can be effective.
- Make full use of court with diagonal spike.
- Good hitting technique and jump-off power are a prerequisite for offense from backcourt.

2 Training Methodology

Volleyball places considerable demands on its students. The intricate nature of the game, the great variety of technical and tactical plays for playing game situations successfully, and the demands for team play during constantly changing game phases make a long-term, systematic training programme necessary.

The objective of the training process is varied and can be characterized as follows:

- It consists of the acquisition and game-related adaption of individual and collective plays necessary for the successful play of the game. Tactical aspects are given prime consideration. This then has as its consequence in arranging the various elements and aspects of training programmes.
- Players should concentrate at first on building a diverse repertory of specific skills related to the technique and co-ordination aspect of the game.
- Game plays are further characterized by the close interaction between psycho-motor process (unity between technique and tactics), thus making various demands on players' reception and processing of information. The tactical and mental aspect of training must be developed systematically as well.
- In the past, teachers and coaches of volleyball often concentrated excessively on improving the quality of motor execution (skill development), and no attempt was made to develop the mental aspects involved. However, all offensive and defensive plays in volleyball are mental decisions. The variety of tactical demands and possible solutions, the wide range of techniques, and the multiform grouping of players within the reference system "teammates - opponents - ball - playing area - target," all emphasize the significance of the psychological aspect of game play. We refer to the psychological processes—perception, imagination, thought planning, and decision-making—as cognitive processes. They are information gathering processes serving to create the 6 steps in game plays detailed above (see Section 1.4).

- Observation and analysis of constantly changing conditions for movement, the anticipation and comparison of motor skills needed to perform, changes in game situations or phases and the mental anticipation of potential results of actions based on these, all enable players to make conscious motor decisions and to take an active part in determining play. The control and evaluation of performance, which occurs through different degrees of the player's awareness, completes the range of important cognitive processes.

The discussion that follows is based on two fundamental premises governing the methodological development of technical and tactical plays:

1. structural breakdown of play into typical game phases, basic situations, and forms of execution of play actions - i.e., organization of the elements of the training content according to demands made by the various elements of play (parts of the play as learning objective); and
2. conscious training of play actions by observing the close link between motor components and the qualitative, cognitive components required for high play performance, such as, perception, anticipation, decision-making, etc..

2.1   Stages of Technical and Tactical Training

Four training stages are fundamental to effective organization of the training process.

Stage One

Learning, improving, and consolidating of volleyball specific motor skills, i.e., basic technical schooling of volleyball players.

Content Characteristics of Training: Learning to obtain a correct mental picture of movement; practising and drilling all forms of movement; concentrating on specific motor sequences under preset conditions of performance, but without tactical demands; practising basic techniques and their variations through multiple repetitions, and in conjunction with the movement to the ball (tempo of movement, distance, direction, two-sided approach); adapting motor skills to conditions in the playing area (court awareness); spatial and temporal co-ordination with teammates during ball handling; consolidating motor skills in view of consistency and accuracy.

Stage Two

Developing, improving, and consolidating game plays for solving specific game tasks for a particular situation under constant conditions.

Content Characteristics of Training: Expanding the scope and freedom of decision-making, developing the ability to take decisions, adapting individual play actions to specific play situations as they arise and combining them into standardized play combinations (action sequences); acquiring tactical knowledge (typical features of game situations and phases, tactical rules, and principles); expanding the repertory of individual game skills and court positioning; development and strengthening of situation-relevant motor actions; exercising primarily in preset, controlled situations and in parts of game phases; tackling tasks which occur in relative isolation: for instance, service or attack following "ball from opponents."

Stage Three

Developing, improving and consolidating plays, i.e., integrated volleyball skills.

Content Characteristics of Training: Application-oriented action in different game situations and game phases (player applies possible solutions taught on his own); tackling unexpected situations; dealing with play tasks in different series of game phases (the transitions must be noted); establishing situations which require creative solutions; creating situations requiring innovative solutions; executing plays under position-specific and function-specific aspects; further development of game plays under increasing physical and psychological stress; familiarizing groups of players and the team, implementing the play concept or specific tactical instructions; practising primarily entire game phases, game complexes, and scrimmage.

Stage Four

Applying complex game play under competitive conditions.

Content Characteristics of Training: These include choosing and implementing individual plays independently; perfecting playing ability by meeting demands at the same time on all components of performance; developing game skills in periods of high physical and psychological stress; developing psychological competitive characteristics (ability to work harder, aggressive play, mental stability) and measuring results achieved in learning the preceding stages.

2.2 Drills and Game Series as Methodical Means for Learning Volleyball

The steps in the development of a player's playing ability as ultimate objective require different emphasis during the various stages of performance development. In all learning phases the process of "creating prerequisites first followed by their application during play" should be noted as a basic principle for all training. This is the starting point for the method of teaching volleyball in modern play, i.e., to combine drills and game series so that finally the full game (six players vs. six players) is learned in stages.

This approach underpins our efforts to move to play as soon as possible. It is of particular importance for children who have a strong desire for play, and who tend to lose interest in drilling if play as a training content is neglected. From the viewpoint of training method this serves mainly to enhance cognitive prerequisites. Thus, the content of volleyball instruction must maintain an effective balance between drills and game series.

While in acquiring simple play skills (Stages 1 and 2) the objective and the nature of drills are more or less known, the players need independently to fulfil varied demands within the framework of the game series which they are unable to anticipate. This constant broadening of skills using drills is not an end in itself; rather, it ensures that players are able to integrate the elements of the game learned separately into normal conditions for play. It is therefore imperative that particular training steps not be considered completed and mastered to perfection. That would impede adaptation and further development of what has been learned under variable conditions.

Drill Progression

In compiling the drill series that follow, we have divided the game into its component structures, all the way down to the particular techniques. To each of them we have assigned a wide range of increasingly competitive drills. We cannot assume, however, that once a specific drill series has been completed, success in learning is automatically guaranteed. The drills provide a particular framework for organization and content. We have therefore refrained from making a specific drill sequence into a teaching programme. The drills are intended primarily to give instructors ideas for organizing training sessions.

Game Series Progressions

The drills in the game series are the heart of the training programme. Whereas the drills in the game series may sometimes be used simultaneously (e.g., serving/bumping), the game and competitive forms can be used in succession, depending upon training levels. At first, players will only be able to receive and process a limited amount of information. We shall therefore restrict ourselves to simple game forms. In addition to the official competitive forms we shall use a series of intermediate methodical steps to make completion of skills in the game easier and ensure the continuity of play.

As actions become more complex, freedom in decision-making increases from game to game. While it is important to follow the rules of the six-on-six game in all the game and competitive forms, rules must be adapted to the players' skills and abilities. It is also important to distinguish between the actual competition and exhibition games, scrimmages, and half-court games. Victory is not the object of exhibition games, for example, and players should simply be required to fulfil tactical tasks, with the coach in an advisory and control capacity.

2.3   Sequence of Skills to be Learned

Subsequent chapters will describe learning skills in the sequence they occur in the game. For a general orientation, however, we have chosen another sequence of steps.

1. *Throwing and catching* along with court movement are the basic requirements for initial volleyball training. In addition, drills with different types of balls, "miniature games" that teach athletic co-ordination, and ball over the rope and ball over the net drills can be taught.

2. The most important element in volleyball is *the overhead pass* (see Section 3.3). Players learn best to practise and perfect overhead passing in a "1 on 1" game form. They learn to complete passes within specific court boundaries and in relation to the volleyball net, and develop important psychological skills (visual/motor timing, peripheral vision, "feel" for the ball, alertness, temporal anticipation, and so on).

In this second step, however, it is essential that players learn passing with changes in direction, the normal use of the overhead pass. At this stage passing on court and setting should also be combined. Passing with changes in direction should be practised in two-on-two game style. The complex differences between passing and passing on court, setting and the set pass should become apparent. This will increase the complexity of decision making and co-operation between players.

3. In the third step the *underarm serve* is introduced, while the overhead pass continues to be used in receiving, setting, making the passes, and for defence on court. Although the specific forms of movement of these plays are not yet used, their typical nature may be worked out during the course of play. Players at this stage can begin preparing for the spike (approach and jump), but for now we shall concern ourselves with the two-handed set pass, first as a stationary and later as a jump pass, under competitive conditions.

The main training form is the "2 on 2" style, which is also the first official competitive form. (The variation "3 on 3" may also be used with what has been learned already.) This provides a transition to the next steps.

4. *The increasing offensive nature of the game skills and the differentiation of the defensive elements* are characteristic of the fourth step. The main objectives are learning *the overhead serve* (floating serve, and tennis serve), *the service receive* (bumping), *the spike* (as well as spiking on the stand and then easy spike from the jump), *the one-hand jump set pass*, and *defensive digging* for court defence. *Block defence* using a single-player block should also be mastered and *the back set* should expand the overhead passing repertory. Emphasis must be placed on developing the correct physical skills. Otherwise, chances are that the game plays will be learned incorrectly.

As in the first step, throwing drills (serving, attack) are used. Players on both left and right sides learn defensive techniques (rolling, diving, falling).

More time should be allowed for learning these new elements of the game (court defence, offence), so that complex practising and practising of related game phases can be implemented successfully.

The playing form used is "3 on 3". Co-ordination or team play is fundamental here, and will become more important as we approach the "6 on 6" game. The basic concepts in group tactics in offence and defence should also be mastered at this stage.

5. The fifth step extends the objectives found in the one preceding. Although the spike should not be used extensively in "3 on 3" form, players should now work on it in a systematic and global manner (hitting variations, using the block, etc.).

The prime concern here, however, is *the intelligent use of tactics* as opposed to the aggressive offensive play. Technical demands are broadened in connection with the tactical demands of a new "4 on 4" style. Net play (spike, block) and defensive skills should become more varied with new game skills and specific variations (attack coverage, block coverage) should be introduced. As long as spikes are not yet hit hard, players should attempt to recover the ball as much as possible by moving into proper defensive positions. It is especially important here to practise the interaction block/defence (positional play, orientation towards the block).

Additions to the repertory of techniques in this stage include: *learning the lateral recovery of the serve* , *passes on court* (bump or volley), as well as initial attempts at using *simple forms of attack sets* (preparing for simple offensive combinations).

6. The sixth step brings us to "6 on 6" form of practice, and it is here that the entire diverse range of game plays and group tactics are learned. All factors in the game plays which have an effect on performance must be perfected here parallel to one another. The last new fundamental game element that appears here is *the two-player block*. It should now be possible to play "6 on 6" successfully. All other game components may now be worked out in relation to training levels of the players, as well as individual and collective tactical demands. It would be appropriate here for the coach to develop a general progression for learning, a teaching plan. We therefore refer readers to the remarks in Chapters 3-5, where all the elements in the game that go beyond basic requirements are progressively introduced. The game and competitive forms previously mentioned and the additional game styles for use in training are found in Chapters 5 and 6.

2.4   Progressions and Drill Contents

The collection of drills is geared exclusively to tactical and technical training with the purpose of training players to perform under game-like conditions. The collection therefore contains exercise forms that promote skills and play forms related to play action and teamwork in typical game phases. The collection should be seen as a supplement to existing standard literature. Many questions in training activities (planning, organization of practice sessions, athletic training, etc.) are not treated, and mentioned only in passing.

The material has been divided on the basis of several main learning principles. This division should prove useful in organizing a series of drills.

- *Learning the execution of individual game skills, including drill progressions.* The relevant drill series will be found in Chapter 3. The end of each drill series lays the foundation for the next drill series.
- *Perfecting and consolidating individual game skills in connection with previous and succeeding plays (pass/spike/block/defence, etc.).*When practising the plays in complexes, it is important for players to deal with typical situations at first before they concentrate entirely on whole game phases including the components of transition from one phase to another. The drills for both of these main complexes will be found in Chapter 4.
- Perfecting and consolidating individual game skills under competitive conditions.

The training progressions, various modified game forms, and competitive forms are found in Chapters 5 and 6. Drills for training specific situations (saving net balls, spiking of overset balls, attack from backcourt) and a few examples of drills for specific physical training are included among the drill material.

A summary of skills and game plays and patterns to be learned is presented in Diagram 4.

2.5   Game-Like Practice Arrangement

Regardless of the level of volleyball played, the game is not a series of isolated skills strung together, but involves the playing and resolution of game situations and the progression of specific game phases. The drills below reproduce these situations and phases and provide opportunities for developing techniques and tactics, as well as physical and psychological alertness.

Diagram 4   A summary of movement forms and skills, plays and patterns, and training progressions.

Game Skills (Technical Elements)	Game Situations

- Underarm serve;   Serve;

- Overhead serve (tennis serve);

- Overhead serve (floating serve);

- Side arm floating serve;

- Hook serve with spin;

- Service receive (in front of body);   Service receive;

- Service receive (from the side);

- Service receive (falling);

- Service receive (overhead);

- Overhead pass (forward set, straight   Pass (set, court pass);
  overhead and back, in falling, jump posi-
  tion, diagonal from court - specific passes;
  bumps and volleys, direct court pass);

- Spike;   Attack/set pass;

- Stationary/jump set pass;

- Hitting variations (offspeed, tips, twist the
  upper body, wrist only, across the body,
  hook);

- Block (one-, two-, or three-player block);   Attack and zone block;
                                                Court defence (attack
- Defensive dig or bump (two-armed, sta-   coverage).
  tionary, falling, one-hand stationary and   Block coverage, net balls;
  falling)

Game Phases	Training Progressions (Practice & Competitive Forms);
1. Service receive - specific passes or attack sets - attack;	• Ball over the rope; • Ball over the net (with catching, with double play);
2. Service receive - high parallel passes - attack;	• Playing style "1-on-1"; • Playing style "2-on-2"; • Playing style "3-on-3" (mini
3. Passes on court after easy ball from opponent - specific passes and attack sets - attack;	volleyball); • Playing style "4-on-4; • Playing style "6-on-6";
4. Block rebound - defence/passing on court - specific passes/attack sets - attack;	
5. Bypassing block - defence on court - high parallel passes/attack sets - attack;	
6. Service receive - high diagonal passes - attack;	
7. Spike past block - defence on court - high diagonal passes from back court - attack;	
8. Spikes deflecting off block - defence/passing on court - high passes/attack passes - attack;	
9. First ball attack (oversets);	
10. Attack from backcourt (as broken play in attack combinations, deliberate attack with high passes);	

The following list of a few teaching rules should ensure effective practising under game-like conditions.

● Setting a Game Task

The drill should be based on a more or less simplified game situation corresponding to the game and game task. Players have to perform this task using the appropriate techniques and tactics.

● Practising from Play-Related Positions

The players exercise in correct spacial relationship to the net and line up in a formation corresponding to the play situation.

● One Main Play as the Focus of the Drill

The content of the drill should incorporate one main action/play related to the game situation and the objective of play. While players and the coach are concentrating on this action, they should not neglect supporting actions, movements, and plays; players and coaches should concentrate on this game phase while executing auxiliary plays.

● Arrangement of Preceding and Following Plays

In the drill the main play action should be preceded and followed by plays corresponding to the game situation (see mandatory actions). This main play is executed as a link in a chain of actions applied to players and the team. Plays with and without the ball are combined.

● Game-Like Speed and Dynamics

When practising, players should move just as they would in the game situation. The main play in particular should always be executed with game speed and dynamics. Positional play and control of the playing area and motion without and towards the ball based on the essential situations should be developed to game standard.

● Game-Like Co-operation

The drill should be arranged so that, for the main action/play at least, co-operation and team work among several players is in keeping with game play. Organized collective action is especially important for defence and coverage assignments. In order to avoid misunderstandings, the coaches should discuss the plays with the athletes.

● **Organization of Drill with "Opponent"**

The drill should contain an active or passive opponent played by the coach or other team members so that the action may be influenced directly by the "opponents'" moves. An opponent may begin or end the series of plays or the opponent may be incorporated into the sequence. (Example: server begins drill, then attacking team spikes towards one position.)

● **Flexible Drill Structure**

The drill should not be done mechanically. A flexible arrangement is essential for the development of playing ability. Players adapt to the great variety of situations and are compelled to make tactical decisions and must execute diverse skills. Changes in game tasks, or principal actions, by modifying drills or increasing complexity, require and develop mental agility in players (ability to switch to another activity).

● **Measurable Results**

The drill should contain a measurable objective for the principal action/ play or series of plays, whose fulfilment can be assessed by the players themselves. With the assistance of the coach, technical and tactical accuracy may be evaluated using criteria such as motor performance, sureness and precision of execution, hitting target areas, etc. Working with reference points, goal markers, target areas, and similar increases the effectiveness of training.

2.6   Role of the Instructor/Coach in Drill Organization

Training should closely approximate competitive play by emphasizing and reproducing game conditions in the drills. For this, coach-oriented or ordered drills may be necessary, especially at the lower training levels, but also where advanced players are concerned. Coaches must exert "appropriate pressure" concerning:

- execution of the drill;
- execution of the game phase;
- deciding which skills to use;
- variation in skills and in motor execution;
- correct technical execution;
- motivation, mobilization of energy and positive reinforcement of

players.

Coaches assume a central role in many drills and must be able to use many ball handling techniques in order to ensure that the objective in each drill is fulfilled. The "coaching technique" must be thoroughly mastered. It includes the following skills:

- hitting serves;
- spiking, throwing ball into play, passing, and setting;
- receiving the ball, passing/defence on court;
- spiking from platform for attack;
- feeding and spiking ball into play.

In this active role, coaches should impress upon the drill their methodical training plan and create the conditions under which the game task is to be completed. Training quality will improve considerably than would be the case if players were exercising exclusively among themselves. This holds true even right up to elite performance training.

2.7   Effective Coaching Tips

Success in coaching is not automatically guaranteed by the number of drills or the amount of time spent in training. Optimum learning is distinguished by successful and quick mastery of the material. Paying attention to learning rules and instructions serves as an orientation aid in designing a more effective training process. The following tips refer particularly to: (a) developing a willingness to learn; (b) creating further objective and subjective conditions for learning; (c) designing the content of tactical and technical drilling; (d) and planning the subject matter and the processes for information-receiving and information-processing during a play (including evaluation and feedback).

Creating Desire to Learn

- A strong desire to learn is necessary if the material is to be mastered. Mere repetitive drills without correct attitudes and motivation cannot lead to success.
- Learning engendered through a fear of punishment or embarrassment, or which takes place under pressure or when symptoms of fatigue are present, will be unsuccessful. Practise, therefore, under relaxed conditions. Praise and rewards will motivate learners in general better than

criticism.

- Different types of achievement tests and competitions help to promote a willingness to learn and accelerate progress in learning, but they should not be overemphasized at the beginning of the learning process.
- The relationship between coach and athlete affects the learning process. It is especially important to speak a common language, to find the same meaning for the same words. Since coaches observe, judge, and counsel athletes during play as well as evaluate their results, they can provide players with insights into the correlations between plays and foster interest and a willingness to fulfil new objectives.

Creating Further Objective and Subjective Conditions for Learning

- Work through the material step by step and increase the level of difficulty of the drills gradually. Setting goals which can be reached leads more frequently to success and maintains interest in practising. Experiences of failure — the result of demands which are too high — hinder the learning process.
- Organize training in a flexible manner. Avoid causing fatigue among players by alloting small rest periods. Drills that are one-sided lead to monotony and mental satiation, both of which hinder the learning process. Overcome this danger by changing the objective (providing a new task to learn) and by providing new or additional stimuli (using different balls, raising the net, target requirements, etc.)
- Distributed learning (particularly for young beginning players) is better than massed practice. It is better to distribute new material over relatively short drill phases (20-30 min per unit of training) and to allow for rest periods in between rather than trying continually to master new ideas over a relatively long period of time, i.e., 1-2 hours per unit of training.

  Active rest periods promote learning. Mental activity (verbal evaluation and mental repetition of what was practised) aids in entrenching what was learned.

  Short drill phases prevent symptoms of fatigue from occurring; the principle "only drill until symptoms of fatigue (decreasing accuracy in play) appear" holds true for distributed learning.

Tips for Planning the Learning Material and for Designing the Elements of Technical and Tactical Drilling

- A systematic and thorough basic technical training (learning fundamental motor skills) is essential.

- All-round, general physical preparation is also necessary for success in learning in the technical and tactical areas.

- Learn the motor skills as much as possible as a whole. Familiarize yourself first with various parts (segments) of the motor skill and then practice it actively in its totality as soon as possible.

- Depending upon the material, learning may be organized in "parts" or as a whole. The method to be used will depend upon the point of reference (e.g., practising a game phase falls under learning as a whole, but it can also be considered as "learning in parts").

- A knowledge of motor skills aids in athletes' own learning process. Use the movement sequences illustrated (below and in the diagrams in the pictorial appendix) to acquire mental perceptions of the movements. A practical demonstration is restrictive and inadequate because the motor skills are usually executed too quickly.

- Introduce players to theory and its applications (technical and tactical areas) gradually. Simplified drills, complex drills, game situation drills and finally competitive play drills form a natural progression in learning the newly presented theoretical aspects of the game.

- Pay close attention to the main features in the motor skills and always check technical and tactical training using simple evaluation methods.

- Make the game situation drills the core of the training process. Incorporate the idea of the "big game" or "important point" as much as possible in all modified types of competition. However, adapt the game rules to players' training levels.

- Use individual drills (i.e., without coach, and/or drills off the wall) in preparation for technique training and as an additional means of making training flexible (special warm-ups, getting used to the ball, co-ordination training).

- In technical training (mastery of the gross form of the motor skill) adopt game-style drills as soon as possible and set tactical tasks. Use the tactical rules given in association with the range of drills and use the rules provided in Section 2.5.

- Intensity and scope of technical and tactical tasks largely determine the level of difficulty of the drills. They should be so organized that each drill task is solved with a maximum degree of accuracy. Overtaxing players means they will learn game plays incorrectly.

- Coaches/instructors must control the intensity (pace, number of repetitions, length of rest periods) of the tasks, especially for beginners. Special attention must be given to the objective in learning and players' training levels.

- When learning motor sequences the initial objective is not to complete as many repetitions as possible. It is much more important to combine actual initial practical trials and mental activity with the sequence just carried out (fault corrections, refining perception of movement).

- In principle, when practising technique and co-ordination, as many repetitions maybe used as is feasible without reducing motor accuracy.

Requirements

Prevent fatigue with beginners; demand motor accuracy of experienced players even when fatigue is present; set number of repetitions according to intensity of movement.

- When practising attack, blocking and court defence, which are particularly intensive play actions, practising in short spurts (approx. 10 repetitions, 30-60 sec each) with brief rest periods during or after the series. (Interval principle: ratio of rest periods to drill should be from 1:2 to 1:4). When working on serve, service receive, court passing, and setting, accuracy is the prime consideration. Continuous play with numerous repetitions is a predominant feature of the drill.

- In complex drills, game phase drills, and practise games (e.g., two-on-two, three-on-three), coaches aim at arranging the drills with an emphasis on competition. The alternation between long and short drill periods, the execution of movements of varying intensity and the rest periods are determined to a large extent by the character of the play practised. When using different types of drills and scrimmages, coaches can control the intensity of training by feeding the balls themselves at various speeds.

- Once the sequences of movements are mastered they can be improved and strengthened by frequent and "intense" learning. This applies, for instance, in teaching concentration endurance when practising serve receives (longer drill duration without decrease in accuracy).

- In designing training programme make sure to combine tactical and technical play actions—typical for volleyball—with demands on speed and speed/strength, and coordination.

- Review repeatedly the material that you have already mastered. At the beginning of each practice session practise the main elements of several or at least the last drill in a progression before commencing a new drill.

- When arranging material for a training programme take advantage of positive transfer, i.e., the positive influence of one group of movements on another.

- The basis for this positive transfer is flawless technique training (because of difficulties of retraining of incorrect motor sequences).

Only material that players have down pat can be used and thus transferred.

- The more two actions are similar, the greater the transfer.
- The transfer effect is greater from a more difficult drill to an easier motor skill than vice versa.
- "Right-left transfer" plays a major role in training new skills (principle of using both sides). At the beginning practise using only one side.

Tips for Effective Use of Individual Cognitive Processes During Game Plays

Observation, Perception, and Analysis of Game Situation

- Information-receiving involves differentiating, identifying, and recognizing pieces of information. When arranging training, always start from the assumption that the large amount of information in a game must be dealt with gradually.
- The following principle holds true: "Proceed from the most basic to the most difficult." Limit the amount of information at first. Set the drill task clearly, stress the most important cues and explain the significance of these cues for solving the task or performing a skill.
- A knowledge of the characteristics of the game situations and its phases (spatial/temporal, court awareness and its relation to motor skills) and the flight of the ball (path, speed, spin, direction) simplify locating and recognizing important cues.
- Have players distinguish first between aspects of the game that are completely different, then gradually between ones that are more similar. Help players by detailed explanation and allow them to make their observations.
- With the aid of past experience and knowledge they have already gained, players can identify important aspects more rapidly and directly. Pieces of information with a specific meaning, such as motor governing signals, are decisive in regulating all further activity.

Mental Solution of Game Situation

- Decision-making processes are at the heart of information-processing (choosing between important pieces of information, establishing relationships between this information, planning execution/motor programme).
- The basic conditions for correct decision-making involve several possibilities or alternatives, a knowledge of their use for fulfilling the objectives and of the importance of these objectives themselves, as well as determining the probability of realizing an alternative.

- Coaches not only provide athletes with information necessary for decision-making (e.g., tactical rules), they also attempt to improve decision-making ability in practical training. They should:

(a) increase or decrease the quantity of information relevant to decision-making;
(b) vary sources of information;
(c) create situations requiring a conscious decision and not only unconscious reactions; and
(d) create situations requiring decisions matching to the players' decision-making and motor abilities.

Motor Solution of Game Situation

- Combine practising motor skills with theoretical instruction to facilitate a correct conception of the movements (use picture series, filmstrips, instructional cards, error diagrams, etc.). It is unwise, especially when developing complex techniques, to begin immediately with direct practice, which leaves much to trial and error.
- Stages where specific motor sequences were learned must be followed by a stage of varied training (e.g., after learning the spike practise high ball attack, first ball attack, attack from backcourt, attack with different passes, etc.).
- Use various aids (target demands, accoustic information - "extended arm," "hand clenched") to enhance the quality of performance.

Evaluation and Correction of Game Plays

- Players have three possible evaluation methods: feedback about movement sensations or "muscle sense"; comparison between theoretical goal and execution; and comparison of their own assessment with coach's corrections.
- Movement execution is always the result of the previous steps. Coaches must analyze and understand the result and its causes, and include the player in question or everyone involved in the analysis. An evaluation of the various ways in which the situation may be resolved is important.
- Do not merely isolate the mistake when incorrect decisions are made. Together with the player, try to find the cause of the error that has lead to an incorrect analysis of the situation and an improper assessment of the utility of particular actions. It is essential to ask players about the reasons for their decisions.
- In tactics training, do not correct individual motor skills, but rather the

mental resolution of the game situation (accuracy of decision regarding objective with the relevant motor skill). Errors in technique are most often the result of mistakes in the first and second phases of learning.

- Beginners must be made aware of the difference between an incorrect motor skill already carried out and the correct way of its execution.

- Optimum correction is possible when the player compares his own performance of movement with ideal execution in the related situation. The comparison should be made immediately and in a manner the player can cope with; correct information of the error should be followed by a newly set task.

- Merely determining an error is not sufficient because the player is unable to link this information with his sense of movement. Positive reinforcement of correct execution is essential: it helps develop a player's "good feel for movement." Mental practice and execution cannot improve until players have realized the causes of their mistakes and compared them with their impressions of the movement.

- Also correct errors by providing players immediately with diametrically opposed situations (e.g., jumping too early for a spike should be corrected by beginning the approach after considerable delay).

- Reinforcement and praise are not necessary after every successful trial, but should be spaced apart reasonably. Positive recognition given too frequently hinders learning; players forget more quickly what they have learned. With beginners, occasional praise and stress on correctly-performed technique (play action) amid a number of faulty actions contribute to the learning success.

3 Learning the Game

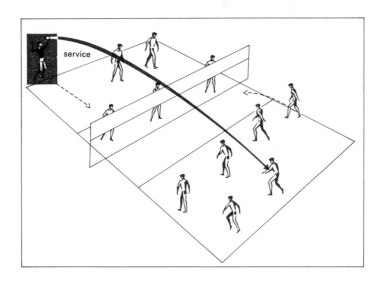

3.1 The Serve

3.1.1 General Characteristics

The serve is made after a previous interruption in play and initiates a new series of actions. After the referee has blown the whistle the player has five seconds to hit the serve. It involves, of course, a fixed serving area, but players have the freedom to choose the serve style he is most comfortable with and individual tactical decisions regardless of group tactics. A serve can be made easily using a simple serve style, such as underarm serve. The use of the serve by seasoned players is however associated with a variety of technical and tactical requirements.

The serve begins the offensive play: an individual player can score points directly without help by others. However, any serve fault results in loss of serve for the serving team. Both situations influence morale. Re-

member that when players avoid mistakes, an efficient serve can make it more difficult for the opponent to launch a counterattack. Only use serves you have mastered. *Certainty goes before risk.*
The *underarm serve* is the style preferred among beginners. At first it is used to put the ball into play, but it should also be hit with a tactical objective. It is easy to learn and should belong to each player's repertory of skills.

The *overhead serve* with spin is an offensive serve and is similar in execution to the spike. Its use involves risk and thus it should be used only when it is tactically justified (scoring, receiving line spread far across court, poor lighting conditions, etc.). Ill-considered use of this serve only undermines tactical discipline.

When using the *hook (or roundhouse) serve* success depends entirely upon the force of the shot. It is a purely offensive serve and can rarely be hit in a specific direction. It is intended merely for attack and cannot easily be placed. As it involves higher error risk its application needs even stronger justification than that indicated for the overhead serve.

The *frontal and lateral floating serve* are execution styles without spin. They are characterized by the irregular path of the ball. They can be hit with great accuracy and dominate all of the variations used.

The course of the game depends mainly on different variations of service which are selected according to each situation. Each player should master two types of service, one for power, the other for acuracy. If players have mastered these variations, this causes stress on the opponent players who must always be prepared for new situations and, in so doing, expend a major portion of their mental energies (concentration) which eventually leads to errors. Unfortunately, this is not sufficiently exploited by many teams. Furthermore, the same type of serve can be varied, always creating different conditions for receiving the ball (e.g., variations in positioning the ball, velocity, and flight curve).

3.1.2   Teaching the Serve

Throwing different sized balls across short and long distances is appropriate as a preparatory drill for learning how to serve. Execution is similar to serving styles. Players should be taught first how to toss the ball for the serve: (a) underarm serve: to the right in front of serving arm; (b) tennis serve: towards the body and over the right shoulder; (c) hook serve: with both hands in front of body above head and over the right shoulder, ball must drop to floor in front of body; (d) floating serve: ball thrown into play flat without spin. Practising the striking arm action with a stationary ball (pendulum ball) also aids in the learning process by allowing players to adopt the correct position in relation to the ball when it is held at a height that corresponds to its movement under normal conditions. Learning the correct serve movements is continued in the following series of drills which, in principle, can be used for all types of serve. The players start exercising under simplified conditions to be able to concentrate fully on visualizing movement structure. It is especially important during this stage in training for coaches to identify and correct wrong movements and to demonstrate the correct movements. Team members should practise serving over the net and then gradually increase distance. Serving the ball directly to the partner now also requires achieving the right flight path. As soon as players can serve the ball from the serving area over the net, target requirements can be set.

3.1.3   Coaching Tips

The mastery of movement sequence does not signal the end of specific service training. Maintenance of individual serving styles, the consistency of the skill, and the ability to hit a desired target on a first attempt with varying amounts of power can only be achieved if a portion of training time is devoted solely to this objective. Players should practise the serve for at least five minutes during each session. This should be done at the beginning of a practice if the emphasis is on game and competitive styles or if accurate serve is essential for the continuous flow of the drills. Service practice between strenuous drill components (especially jumping) is also recommended. This ensures rest periods are used effectively. A series of serves without tactical requirements or to fixed targets are suitable for consolidating sequences in the service movement. Competitive drills (whoever hits ten serves first in a row, without faults, etc.) offer additional stimulus for intensive practice.

Players should practise serving on both sides of the court. It is also important to serve as much as possible to marked locations on the court.

These training rules can be instilled through the drills that follow. The tactical framework of practice is created by fixing specific tasks (e.g., alternation between short/long serves) on the basis of tactical rules and also by using the appropriate serving variation to solve these tasks.

These activities enable players to prepare themselves efficiently for the requirements of the game, to choose from different tactical variations and to determine the goal to be reached. Practising should now involve more complex drills, game, and competitive forms. At this stage in training, serves must be hit to specific targets; players unable to do so cannot bring all the factors required for effective serve into realization.

While the drill series that outlines teaching the serve primarily develops the sequences of arm motion and hitting specific target areas, the emphasis in the remainder of the drills is on independent determination by players themselves of the objective and selection of the service style. Coaches must then create situations that call for the direct use of specific tactical rules. They should still set the objectives for beginners and should also intervene by verifying the results obtained. They must criticize the plays constructively and instruct players as to how they may meet the objective better by changing the service style. Experienced players are able to perfect on their own how their serve should be used, by drawing both on their technical facility and on their knowledge of different tactics.

3.1.4   Tactical Rules

- Concentrate before making the serve (let other teammates retrieve ball): (1) watch opponents; (2) establish the target; (3) concentrate while making contact.
- Stay behind the base line and ensure the ball is thrown correctly.
- Do not make two consecutive service faults. After one service fault the next one must be a good one.
- Never miss serves: (1) at beginning of set, (2) at end of a set (3) after a time-out, (4) after a substitution, and (5) when under exceptional mental stress.
- Accurate serves are, for the most part, better than power serves, which are full of risk. Power serves should be used only when the risk entailed can be justified tactically (e.g., when opponents have a strong offensive line). Careless mistakes undermine tactical discipline.
- Serve the ball to specific opposing players (to player who just made a mistake, to weaker players, to player who just entered the game, etc.).
- Against teams with strong service receive serve the ball to open areas of the court and in between players.
- Take advantage of holes and mis-alignments in the receiving formations. Also direct serves to path of back-row setter.

3.1.5   Drill Pool

Preparatory drills: D 1 to D 3.
Application of serve drills: D 4 to D 12.

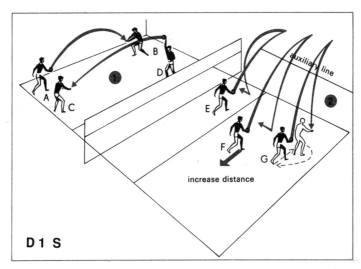

D 1 S

D 1

Preparing for the serve 1: Develop accuracy by using the appropriate amount of strength. 2: Concentrate on throwing the ball correctly, take correct position in relation to the ball and time your strike well.

Hitting the ball directly to partner using different serving techniques A net is not used; a three-metre high cord is suitable. Emphasising accuracy helps players to develop a "feel" for the right amount of power.

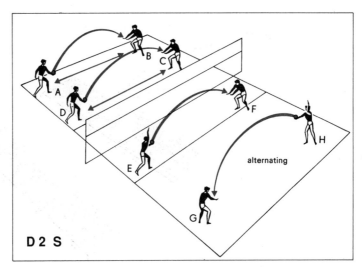

D 2 S

D 2

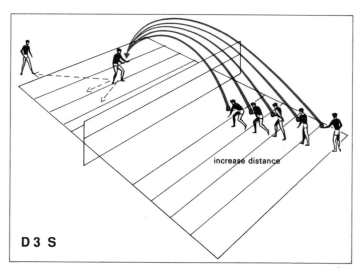

D 3

D 3 S

Learning to serve at increasing distances from the net. Hit ball accurately in order to achieve the proper flight path. As soon as players can serve from the serving area, begin combining drills with tactical demands.

Developing serving accuracy. Use both short and long serves to hit target areas. Indicate the kind of serve and the intended location; direct it to a specific area of the court.

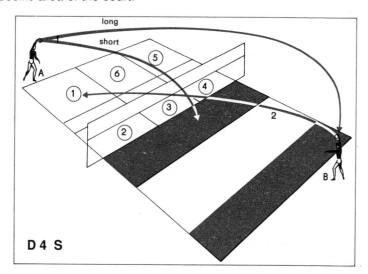

D 4

D 4 S

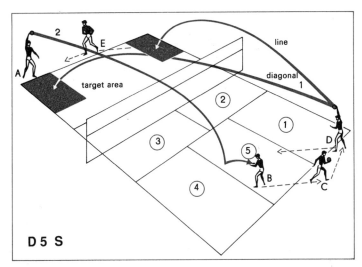

D 5

D 5 S

Developing accuracy and consistency. 1: Alternate between serving along the line and diagonally to the deep corners. Try to hit the target areas. 2: Serve the ball to specific areas on the court.

Serving into open areas between receiving players: Simulate the receiving line; hit serves into areas between players. Tell players where to serve the ball before the service is made.

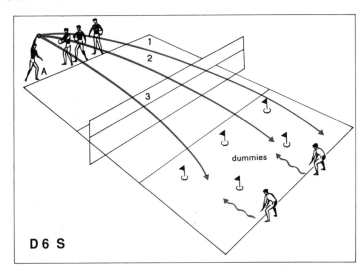

D 6 S

D 6

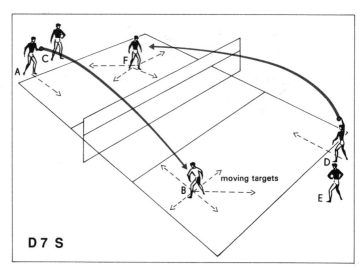

D7 S

D 7

Serving to moving targets. Practise in pairs; alternate between serving and receiving. Receiving player always changes position. Serve should be hit correctly on the first attempt.

Serving at moving targets. Player C constantly changes position on court. Serve directly to the receiver, without making errors. Develop a feel for the right amount of power when hitting the serve.

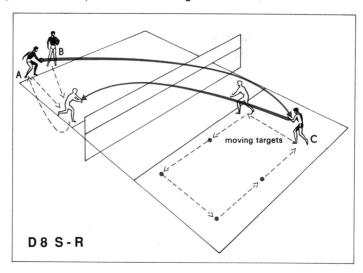

D8 S - R

D 8

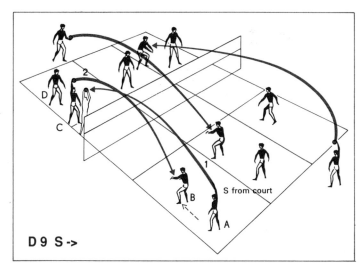

D 9

D 9 S ->

Serving game. Serve from back of court - pass the ball high toward net; good service and fault by receiver 1 point; service fault but successful pass = 1 point for receiving team; normal rotation, or rotate after 5 serves.

Serving relay. Serve accurately - catcher must remain in target area. Each ball caught in target area scores 1 point. After catching serve, run to serving area. Which team can score 10 points first?

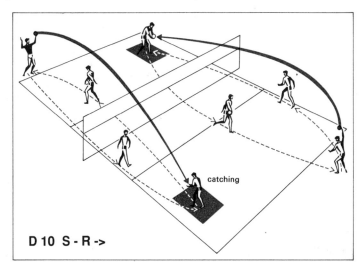

D 10 S - R ->

D 10

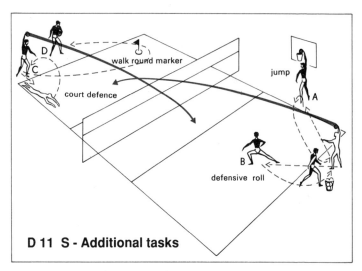

D 11 S - Additional tasks

D 11

Serves with additional tasks. Intensive serving with increasing physical activity. After completing additional physical tasks (at the coach's discretion), pay special attention to concentration phase before serving (use the 5-second rule).

Continuation of play after the serve. Transition to complex exercising. After serving run immediately to a position on court and be prepared for the play action.

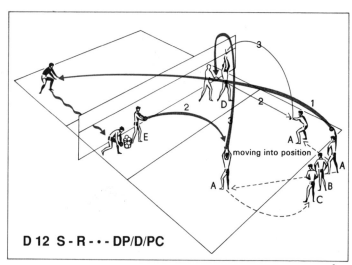

D 12 S - R - · · - DP/D/PC

D 12

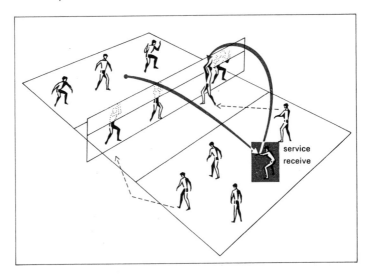

3.2   The Service Reception

3.2.1   General Characteristics

Secure and accurate service receive is the basis for counter-attack. Although the situation appears relatively simple for the receiving players (stationary server; receiving formation can be set up without haste because of previous interruption in play; target is largely determined), beginners in particular experience difficulty in passing the serve accurately. It is precisely at this point that many rallies are often interrupted. At the same time, faults mean a loss of points. If a point is not lost directly, a poor pass at least serves to make counterattack more difficult or even thwarts it completely. If there is too great a discrepancy between serving and receiving, the result is an unsatisfactory play that fails to reach its full potential and remains without any variation or dynamics associated with the game itself. For these reasons, *service reception is a key element in successful play.*

Unflagging attention and a highly developed ability to concentrate are essential when preparing for and receiving the serve. Failure to focus on the serving player properly, a lack of knowledge of the effects of different types of serves and of the appropriate motor responses will mean that the number of faults in receiving a serve will be high. Although the passing of the serve by individual players is crucial, team play among the receiving team indirectly affects success.

The most important types of receiving techniques are recovery using the overhead pass (see Chapter 3.3) and using the underhand pass (bumping). The *overhead pass* is fundamental to beginners' training. It is very useful for reception of underarm serves directly. Bumping is good preparation for movement towards the ball and body position at time of execution, all of which are necessary for recovering difficult balls. (Note: using bumping too early will result in lack of movement on court, which is essential for training defence on the court and for setting.)

As players increase their mastery of serving styles, bumping becomes the main form of receiving the serve. Seasoned players can use it with the same accuracy as an overhead pass. Bearing in mind the dangerous nature of the service it is not advisable to practise only the basic forms of bumping (body in frontal position behind the ball). The play situation often requires sidearm service receive and other variants similar to defending the court while falling. Therefore, practise these rigorously and in a purposeful manner (increasing the scope of action: low, high, sideways).

3.2.2   Teaching Service Reception

Initially motion on the court (forwards, backwards, sideways) is practised. Chief characteristics of these drills are rapid starting from the ready position, quick short steps, and sudden stopping. The activities may be combined with players catching balls fed by the coach. Arms are kept straight at all times. While moving players should squat or crouch down for playing a medium or low pass. Exercising with the ball at rest serves to explain the player's correct position in relation to different types of serves.

To obtain a feeling for the ball the player may balance the ball on his extended arms kept close together. For further practice we refer to the series designed for learning the bump pass. Exercises for defending the serve by the overhead pass may be found in Section 3.3.5.

As in preparatory drills (position to ball, play with ball), individual drills against a wall are effective as in learning defence on court and passing. When practising in pairs (partner tosses the ball into play or hits it to partner) players should first practise passing serve without using the net. (partners stand 6-10 m apart). At the next stage players defend the ball struck over the net; the service then gradually transfers to the service area. Both drills are begun with simple serves so that players learn to receive properly.

Once the players are able to return the ball accurately to their partners, introduce and practice receive of service with change of direction. Players must constantly work with target requirements (passer at net, passing area of back-row setter) in keeping with tactical objectives in recovery of the service.

With team play in service reception formation players proceed from learning the sequences in the movement to improving and consolidating them under game conditions.

In general, the players should make every attempt to keep the ball in their own court while exercising receive of easy and more difficult serves.

3.2.3 Coaching Tips

Being a "key action," service receive requires a major part of training time. While exercising with emphasis on a specific exercise makes great demands on concentration, it does not involve a great deal of physical effort. It is therefore recommended to insert training for receiving the serve, like that for service, between two strenuous exercises. The coach must ensure that the exercises are conducted at a moderate pace and that a great number of repetitions can be made. The forms of exercise can be varied by altering throwing the ball or the serve (trajectory, strength, direction), change of receiving position and varying target demands. Variation is important, even under simplified conditions. In practice a player may often be unable to cope with a ball which he cannot defend by using standard movements (body behind the ball) and so he makes errors. The sooner different tactical requirements are imposed after passing the serve, the easier it is to prevent players from resorting automatically to only one variation or movement when receiving serves.

The coach should make sure that players correct any errors occurring during practice. Movements can be improved and consolidated only if players practise constantly and repeatedly. By familiarizing themselves at the same time with tactical aspects, players can prepare themselves effectively for receiving a serve in a complex drill as well as competition. This is the framework within which players need to perform under constantly changing conditions and act as a well-coordinated team within a larger scope of decision making.

3.2.4 Tactical Rules

- Keep a close watch on the server and note his readiness for movement. Include in your preparation any previous experience you may have had with the opponents (specific features).
- Pass powerful offensive serves in a position similar to that assumed for

defence on court, and, in this way, "cushion" the force of the ball.

- Do not allow serves lacking spin merely to rebound; rather, pass the serve actively (legs straight; arms ready, without striking the ball too high or too far).
- The closer to the net the ball is received, the more horizontal arms must be held.
- Play the ball high into the air in front of the setter, but not too close to the net.
- It is better to bump difficult serves into the centre of the court instead of striving for maximum accuracy at the cost of making mistakes.
- Whoever reacts first or calls for the ball *must* play it. If the ball flies directly in between two players, the following rule applies: "Receive right before receiving left."
- Call balls that are out in order to assist other receiving players. .
- Form receiving formation quickly. For power serves move more together; for easy serves and floating serves spread the line wider apart and form a W formation.
- Do not allow any discussion of errors, but rather try to make receiving formation and the players' own positions conform to the peculiarities of the upcoming serve.
- Try to disrupt the opponent's rhythm by time-outs or substitution when several passing errors are committed.
- Observe the receiving player carefully. Inaccurate service receive often requires a player of the receive line-up to set up the ball from the back of the court.
- Tempting the serving player with a hole in the formation where the ball may be hit cannot be recommended as a general tactic, but it can be used effectively from time to time.

3.2.5   Drill Pool

Preparatory drills: D 13 to D 17.
Drills under simplified conditions: D 18 to D 23.
Service reception drills (individually, two- to five-player groups): D 24 to D 34.

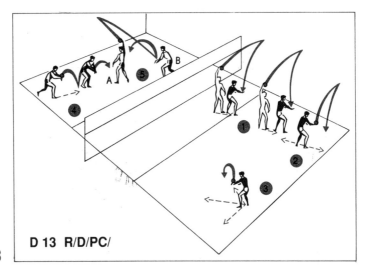

D 13

D 13 R/D/PC/

Diverse preparation for service receive. 1 & 2: Continuous bumping of the ball off the wall. 3: Continuous bumping ball up into air. 4: Bounce ball, run after it, bump it up into the air. 5: Player A shoots ball against wall, and B bumps it to A.

Diverse preparation for passing serve. 1: Bounce ball on floor and dig rebound continuously against the wall (strike the ball on its downward trajectory). 2: Bounce ball and bump it. 3: Make sure the ball is passed to the target area and use correct footwork.

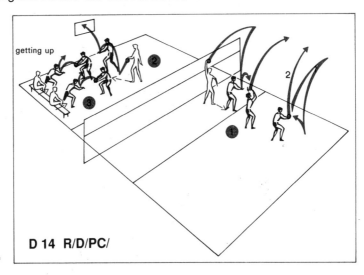

getting up

D 14 R/D/PC/

D 14

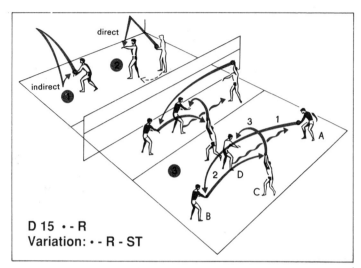

D 15 • - R
Variation: • - R - ST

D 15

Diverse preparation for passing serve. 1: Each time after ball bounces on floor bump it against wall (ball path simulates receding stage of flight path). 2: Bump rebound from wall. 3: Bump ball accurately to partner across short distance.

Prepare for passing serve in pairs. Practise lengthwise on the court; change after 10 serves; play ball high and forwards not too close to the net. Vary service shots from short to long .

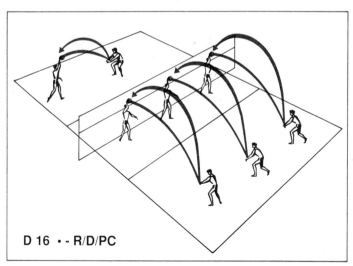

D 16 • - R/D/PC

D 16

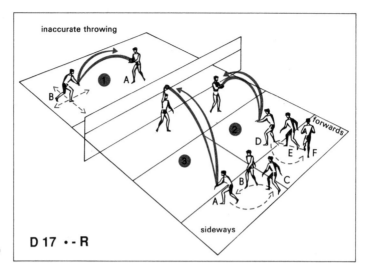

inaccurate throwing

D 17 • - R

D 17

Assume correct position in relation to ball. Vary the toss or hitting of the ball; start from correct distance from ball (do not run up too close to the ball). Remain stationary before you play.

Assume play and receive easy serves. 1: Serve across the net a short distance. Run forwards and bump serve. 2: Player B stands with back to net; after signal he turns quickly and receives the serve.

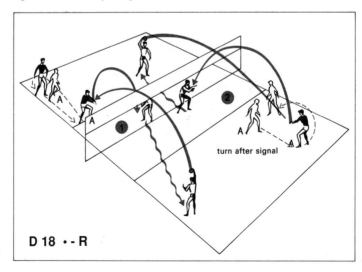

turn after signal

D 18 • - R

D 18

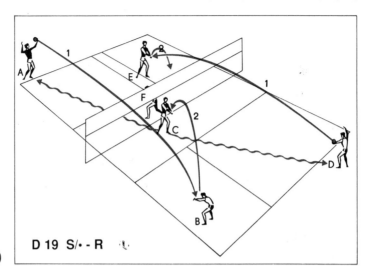

D 19 S/• - R

D 19

Pass serves directly to player C and F. Use easy serves; change after ten serves. Choose a passing position so that you can bump behind ball. Move with the ball and pass using correct footwork.

Prepare for service reception with changing direction. Balls are thrown across a short distance to players B and E. They turn around in direction of play and play to either C or F. Make sure the ball is always in front of you.

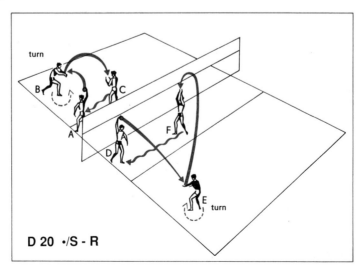

D 20 •/S - R

D 20

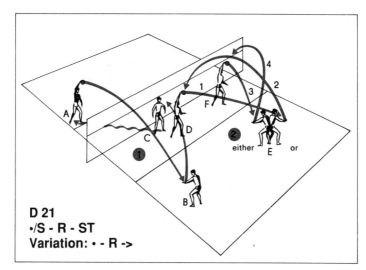

D 21
•/S - R - ST
Variation: • - R ->

D 21

Preparing for service reception under simplified conditions. 1:
Serve is bumped in different direction. 2: Sidearm bump right and left;
players learn to move into play position.

Passing from the side of easy serves. Hit serves into empty areas from
increasing distance. Players B and C use side passing. Make particularly
certain that arms are slightly curved when handling the ball.

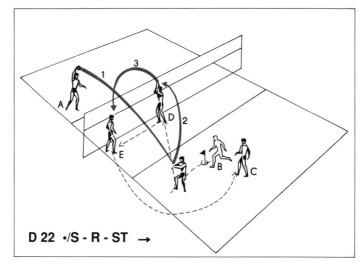

D 22 •/S - R - ST →

D 22

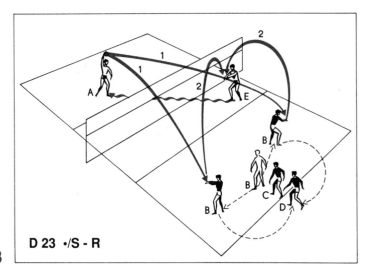

D 23

D 23 •/S - R

Side passing of serve right or left. Use both sides for side reception of serves. Player A hits variable balls either right or left. Player B watches carefully and assumes play position at the appropriate time.

Passing serve close to net. Hit serve to fall close behind net. Players run forward, crouch underneath the ball, and play with arms horizontal. Arm motion provides impulse for ball.

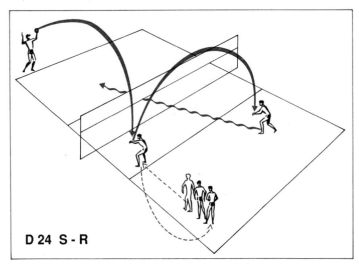

D 24 S - R

D 24

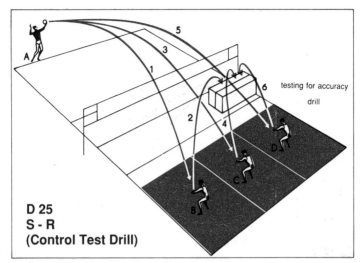

D 25
S - R
(Control Test Drill)

D 25

Check target accuracy when passing serve. Ball is passed toward target from a fixed defensive position. Ball should travel to target with high trajectory and hit target at steep angle of descent. Practise at least ten times at each position.

Passing normal serves with three-player groups. Improve service reception where team play is required. By varying serves receiving line is forced to adapt to new conditions.

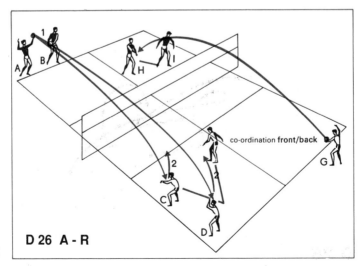

D 26 A - R

D 26

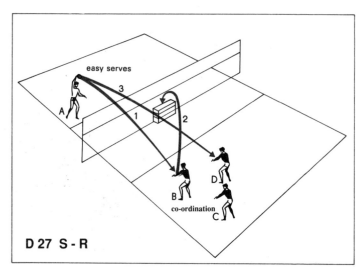

D 27 S - R

D 27

Passing serves in threes. Use easy serves; work emphasizing target accuracy. Ensure team play between front/back players.

Two three-player groups alternate passing easy serves. Serve from back of court; players of three-man line-up co-ordinate their actions calling for the ball; change after five to ten serves, and change position of receiving line at same time.

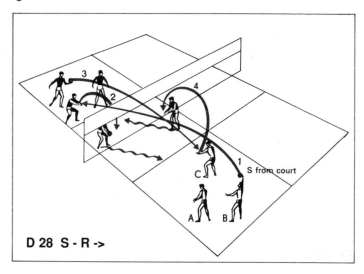

D 28 S - R ->

D 28

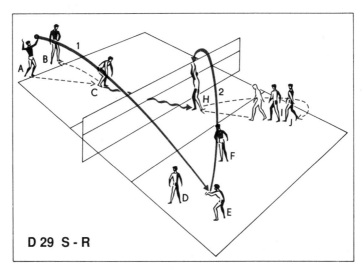

D 29 S - R

D 29

Passing serve to back-row setter with three-player groups. Team play is essential when passing serve with a group of three. Ball is bumped directly to back-row setter's area (between positions 2 and 3). The back-row setter catches ball in proper setting position.

Passing serve to frontcourt passer with four-player squad. Team play between front and back players is important. Make intentions known by calling the ball. Do not stop movement towards ball once already initiated. Setter catches in setting position.

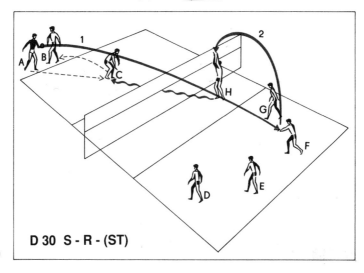

D 30 S - R - (ST)

D 30

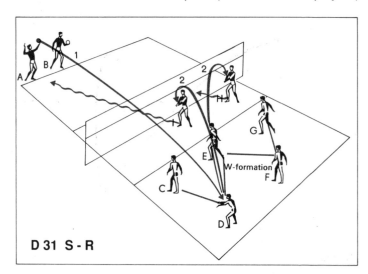

D 31

D 31 S - R

Recovery of serves with five-player squad (W formation). Alternate between power serves (close lined-up) with tactical serves (defensive line spread across court - W formation). Bump to position 3 or 2.

Passing serve - setting. Involves team play between two players in one area. Pass serve over wide distance; change in direction of pass received; set to position 4; keep trunk behind ball, and use correct footwork.

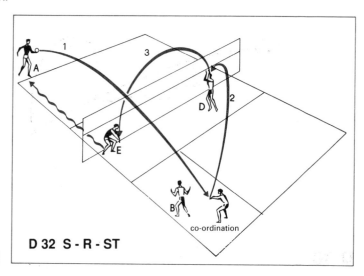

D 32

D 32 S - R - ST

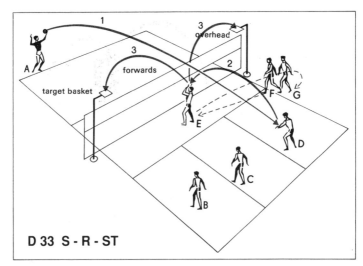

D 33 S - R - ST

D 33

Pass ball to back-row setter - set to target . Bump ball directly to back-row setter's position. If ball is tight against net; set ball overhead backwards. If ball is far away from net, set forward to position 4.

Passing serve and passing on court. The ball is fed to the player receiving serve who then completes the second pass. This drill develops differentiation ability (serve reception vs. easy ball) with movement sequences of similar structure.

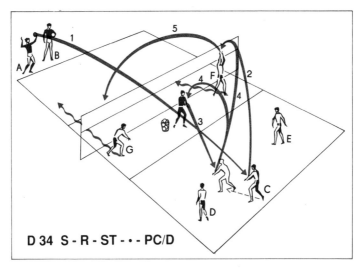

D 34 S - R - ST - • - PC/D

D 34

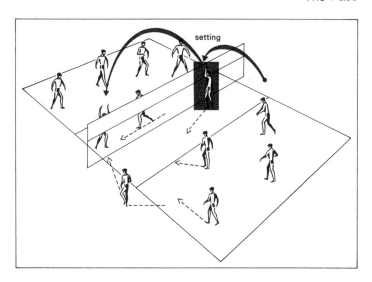

3.3   The Pass

3.3.1   General Characteristics

Passing is the basis of volleyball and forms the core of training for all players. Failure to master passing impedes team play. The pass unites the *two-hand bump* (stationary and falling) as well as the *two-hand overhead pass* (stationary, falling, jump). Included here, of course, is also the *one-hand* pass. All passing plays, by nature, prepare for the attack and have a decisive effect on the further course of events.

We shall differentiate the *first contact* with the ball on the players' half of the court into three types of passing in conjunction with the previous play:

(1) service reception;
(2) defence on court; and
(3) passing on court.

The term passing on court (often referred to as "passing") is used for playing all balls that the opponent is able to hit back over the net or that rebound back from a block and can be easily reached. By its nature this play belongs to defence on the court; target accuracy and precise execution, mainly in the form of overhead passes, are required.

The *second contact* with the ball on the players' half of the court aids in the direct preparation for attack. We refer to it as *set pass for attack* or *setting*. This technique is a central aspect in the game, linking initial plays with the spike. The game sequence shows that at the beginning overhead passing is also used as an offensive play (*set pass*). Overhead passing is therefore the decisive game play in elementary training, and can be used at the same time for receiving, defence on court, setting and attack. Only when players have a better mastery of offensive plays will the forms given be developed, resulting in characteristic movement sequences.

Our extensive treatment of these categories of passing should smooth the way to simple types of games and competitions: a mastery of overhead passing is essential to them. If this is coupled with the underarm serve, the game may now be played according to the rules. We emphasize on thorough training in passing because it helps create conditions for learning important elements: moving towards the ball; determining the proper position in relation to the ball; making accurate plays; using legs correctly during action with the ball; ability to differentiate the game situation while moving; handling irregularly approaching balls; and recognizing the importance of these different elements for the outcome of the game.

In summary, this gradual division in learning the passes, parallel to the training of offensive plays and in conjunction with the games series, is a fundamental principle in volleyball training.

Our prime concern in this chapter is learning the overhead pass. Players must first work through the movement sequence, including movement towards the ball. This will then be combined with the specific forms of "passing on court" and "setting." Emphasis is placed on perfecting the movement sequences under temporal and spatial conditions that are in accordance with the requirements. Although offensive action is still not a factor here (thus diminishing the concerns related to tactical tasks), the tasks set in many of the drills (using variations for passing, determining flight path of ball, motor decisions contingent upon the accuracy of previous action) build towards this. When we consider that the movement sequences required (unlike, for example, catching and throwing) are not part of one's natural "motor skills," and take into account the many variations for passing as well as the considerable demands made on motor accuracy, it becomes evident that difficult tactical tasks would only serve to overtax players.

The most important types of court passes we will learn are the *overhead pass* on court and *underhand pass* on court. Both variations leave players with relatively little leeway for independent tactical decisions. The main requirement is to play the ball directly to a player (a permanent setter at net or into the back-row setter's area) so that conditions exist for mounting an offence. The decision to return the ball immediately following position mistakes by opponent (for example, when a defensive player remains on the floor too long) will rarely be a factor. Using the overhead pass as a *direct pass* for the spike and varying the flight path of the ball high or flat—with the aim of influencing game pace—can be required of more experienced players. Overhead passing on the court is, in principle, identical with the movement sequence when setting.

The underhand pass on the court increases the player's sphere of action; it is more economical in the case of flat balls and also entails less risk in making technical faults. With movement sequences similar to those in receiving a serve, the result is target accuracy equal to that in overhead passing. For beginners, however, it can lead to idleness, and players will be inadequately prepared to use the direct pass.

Setting is often, and with complete justification, referred to as the heart of volleyball. Indeed, it leads to greater specialization of a setter, who is often required to lead the play. This passing variation determines the offense, the accuracy and effectiveness as well as the outcome of the spike. Setters must consider planned offensive plays, and the positioning of both their opponents and teammates. Characteristics of the flight path of the ball (height, distance, direction, speed) will also influence their tactical decisions.

The more information players are able to process and the more variations for passing they master, the greater their scope for action and for making decisions. The elements of the basic motor skill requirements for setting are *forward* and *back passes, parallel* to the net as well as diagonally from backcourt, *lateral passes while rolling over,* and the *bump pass.*

Overhead *jump passes, lateral passes, one-hand overhead jump passes*, and the numerous ways of controlling the flight path of the ball for particular forms of setting are more a part of specific training for those players involved. These types of passes are difficult, both technically and tactically speaking, and their use always depends upon both the play leading up to the set and planned succeeding plays (offensive combinations).

3.3.2   Teaching the Pass

Passing on the court and setting are distinguished chiefly by their various applications. Learning thus occurs as a unified process during the first stage in training. No tactical objectives are set at first in any of the drills. Players should comprehend the movement structure of the pass and practise the sequences, aiming at consistency and accuracy.

First we work out the *running technique* and *orientation on the court.* Suitable drills include running from different basic positions, changing direction and running technique, also combined with simulating the play position. Enjoyable play should be encouraged and various relay plays and "minor games" are suitable for this training.

All further preparatory drills are transferred to the court. The drills at the beginning of Chapter 3.3.5 give a few examples of these, which can be incorporated into the practice session well after the warm-up.

The drills for individual players aid in familiarizing players with important characteristics of passing (position in relation to ball, arm and finger position, etc.). In all the drills given here the ball is almost exclusively thrown by the players themselves or played after it has bounced. In between plays we can practise passing the ball with a spring-like movements of fingers. If each player has a ball, drills against a wall are especially effective. Corrections should be made as to body position at the time of contact with ball, crouching position beforehand and stretching of arms, wrists, and legs. The ball then should be played directly to a specific location and *changes in passing position* should be introduced. Drills become more difficult with the introduction of additional tasks, changing position, and passing the ball with change of direction.

Competitive variations can be used in all of the drills if, for example, a count is made of the number of successful repetitions. This should not be done, however, until the basic movements, for both the upper and lower body, have been mastered flawlessly. The drills for individual players may sometimes also be used in preparation for falling, overhead, and jump pass. Passing drills against a wall can easily be developed into passing relays. Individual drills may also be used for experienced players as part of a special warm-up.

Next, include the partner. Playing the ball or returning it to a partner or the coach is a typical drill for beginners. The player starts with the ball and plays it to a partner or returns balls that were thrown. If a tactical framework has not yet been introduced, direct shots to a partner are an important preliminary stage. As one partner throws the ball, the other becomes accustomed to adapting his performance to the trajectory of the ball. Other suitable drills for organization are initial drills for learning the service receive and court defence.

Two or more players alwasy exercise together, concentrating on movement to the ball and on change of position.

Next, the coach creates exercise conditions typical for training court passes. Players exercise correct court passes to the partner near the net; they react to variably thrown balls, thus approaching the specific forms and conditions of competition. Players learn to differentiate and perform a variation of the system or ball passes by aiming the ball repeatedly at the same target areas from different positions.

Before we combine passing with setting, we should concern ourselves with the *fundamentals of setting*. To begin, players should carry out drills parallel to the net (or along a line), and accuracy requirements should be set when they start passing balls among themselves or passing a ball thrown by a partner. During the next stage the ball is played from inside the court. The setter stands initially in the setting position and moves later to the back-court setter. Throwing the ball at different heights increases the level of difficulty.

Finally, combine all of the requirements into *passing variations with changes in direction*, such that different variations for setting (forward, back, diagonal) are practised continuously and repeatedly. Co-ordinated exercising in groups compels beginners to increase their levels of concentration, since mistakes disrupt this continuous sequence. There are many possible drills, in which *passing on the court and setting* are combined, some of which are complex in nature.

3.3.3   Coaching Tips

When working with beginners, almost the entire practice session is taken up practising passing. In organizing training sessions, remember that the ball does not come to players, but rather players must run to it. Furthermore, note that players almost never play back and forth but rather move in most cases in a different direction from the approach of the ball itself. The various drills given here can be expanded, but within the framework of the drills in this collection. Players should be encouraged to use different types of passes to match the different techniques for feeding or starting the ball into play. Players should proceed very quickly and combine passing with setting. Coaches should help players to execute precise sets or passes. They must organize the accuracy component of passing by setting up appropriate targets etc. as long as there is no subsequent offensive play in the drill. Gradually we give players more information and thus extend their scope of decision-making when opting for ball passing action. This normally requires the coach to devise ball passing exercises so that they closer correspond to later play (increasing the degree of difficulty).

Simple drills for everyone should be a part of every practice session, whether in the warm-up or in the main body of the practice. All players must master these elementary forms. Setting from within the court is often neglected. Specialization among players makes it necessary to do additional drills, so that players are able to complete many movements in succession with maximum accuracy. We feel it is important that passes on court be incorporated into numerous other drills as an introductory element; it offers the opportunity to work specifically on this skill without having to take up additional practice time.

3.3.4 Tactical Rules

It is difficult to judge when a pass is optimal, because clear-cut criteria for such appraisal are lacking. An approximate assessment would entail target accuracy for the play, co-ordination in team play between setter and attacker, as well as the extent to which opponents' weaknesses can be used as criteria. In addition to accuracy, tactical quality is also of prime importance. Whereas decision-making options are limited for passers upon first contact with the ball, many possibilities exist for setting. Inaccuracies and tactical faults when making any of the setting variations only make players uncertain and lead to a loss of game rhythm. On the other hand, good setting can compensate for any previous faults by teammates.

A few tactical rules and principles should help in executing effective passing and setting plays. A framework for setting tasks and objectives for the drills and a variety of criteria for evaluation of the results obtained are provided below.

- During all movements by opponents, do not pay attention only to the approaching ball but observe carefully all preceding actions by opponents(body position, swinging arm motion to set ball on its flight, etc.). The sooner you recognize the path of the ball, the choice of pass, and the tactical plans associated with it, the sooner you can make your own tactical decisions.
- Place body as much as possible behind the ball and turned towards direction of play. Remain stationary and then make pass (run - stand - play).
- For balls that are low and flat, delay your approach, and for high balls with high spin, always pass by bumping.
- For easy balls from opponent use overhead pass as much as possible. The following can be used as a rule of thumb: use overhead pass for balls played over a short distance, underhand pass for balls over a long distance.
- Adapt your play position to the play situation. For passing easy high balls across a short distance, stand in an upright position; for balls started flat or low, use a crouching position.
- You can influence the angle of departure of the ball by changing

position of hands (arms) in relation to the ball. Hands (arms) under the ball should result in a high, steady pass, hands (arms) behind the ball, in a flat, rapid pass.

- Avoid passing when moving backwards; offer your opponent an area in front of you.
- Excluding saves, receive only the balls played into your defensive area.
- A pass begun must be completed, even when a teammate is in a more favourable position to do so. Good co-operation through continuous communication helps to prevent cases of doubt, misunderstanding, and costly mistakes.
- Remember that fast reaction can be at its best if you observe and anticipate your opponents' actions and by getting the proper arm and leg position ready to play. The chief task in passing (as the first contact with the ball) is to create optimum conditions for setting. A few additional rules show how this can be done.
- Creating optimum conditions for setting is especially useful for an attacker, who must pass and then spike to pass the ball at head height for the setter. For this reason, pass high rather than too flat. Experienced players can change game pace effectively from a tactical point of view by altering the flight path of the ball (by playing high balls from opponent quickly and flat forward, or by playing flat balls over a set and high trajectory.
- Never play balls too close to the net and always in front of the back-row setter or frontcourt passer.
- Play a direct offensive pass as a high diagonal pass and in such a way that the attacker is not surprised.
- Direct passes to opponent are not typical of volleyball; use them only in exceptional cases, usually when a position is wide open.

The numerous requirements made for setting means that specialized players are often used for this task. A few general principles and situation-based rules should serve as points of reference for tactically effective setting; ready-made formulas, however, can hardly be prescribed.

- Make passes as simple as possible and choose only those variations of setting you have mastered: accuracy before complexity.
- The more inaccurate the incoming pass, the more simply the ball must be played to the attacker.
- Good offensive play is possible only with good team play between passer and attacker. Try therefore to pay attention to the attacker when

setting. Pass to the attacker who has the best chance of success.
- Try to take advantage of weaknesses in the opponents' frontcourt line and try to disorient their block with screens and feints.
- Always increase the number of variations you know for setting. Be flexible, but always play accurately and consistently.
- When setting the ball do not decide upon a particular attacker; rather, use the entire frontcourt line. During important stages in play take advantage of particular strengths of the spiker first, then play to neighbouring attacker when less complicated conditions are present.
- Make use of the full width of the net when setting.
- Pass the ball so that it ends up in front of the attacker to give him space to swing back his arm and hit the ball.

With setting you can control the pace of the game. This can be effectively achieved by alternating between high, medium high, and flat rapid passes.
- Prepare reliable, steady attacks in critical and unclear situations.
- Accuracy is crucial for high passes. Success in offensive play depends upon the ability of each attacker.
- Flat, rapid setting requires co-ordinated team play between setter and attacker. Rapid combinations as an end in themselves are incorrect tactically.
- A medium high pass forwards and overhead is a useful alternative to fast setting. It may also be played effectively when the first pass has not been played to the net correctly.
- Jump passes are appropriate only if direct passes are used occasionally for second player attacks. Rule of thumb: meet good direct passes with a jump pass, inaccurate passes with immediate attack.
- Play back sets as much as possible at medium height only (more accuracy is required due to loss of visual control).

Players should familiarize themsleves with further technical and tactical rules in underhand passing (no running passes, remaining under and behind ball; playing position and use of body contingent upon height and span of passing). These also apply to setting. In addition, the following should also be observed:

- Change body position as quickly as possible after an inaccurate pass. Watch your teammates and never automatically assume that a direct pass will be made with maximum accuracy.
- When balls fly into play rapidly and powerfully, place hands close together and tighten the fingers, keeping them spread.

- Do not set smaller players too close to the net for the attack.
- Communication before each sequence between the setter and attacker will support good technical and tactical team play.
- Do not play diagonal passes from the backcourt too closely to the net; instead set in front of the attacker, and as far as possible from opponents' previous offensive attack.

These rules are developed further in conjunction with the different playing systems (permanent frontcourt passer, back-row setter sets, and so on). It should be clear that the choice of playing system for the attack depends heavily upon skills of attackers forming the offensive line; for other models consult the relevant literature.

3.3.5   Drill Pool

Preparatory drills: D 35 to D 40.
General passing drills (without tactical framework) : D 41 to D 54.
Setting: D 55 to D 70.
Passing on court drills, combination passing on court/setting: D 71 to D 107.

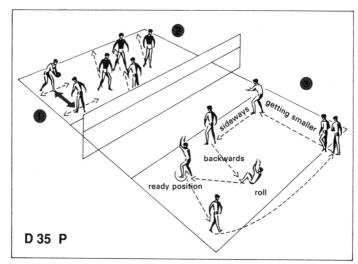

D 35   D 35 P

Movement on court. 1: Remain at same height. 2: "Mirror" drill. 3: Sequence of different movements with specific playing positions.

Determining arm and hand position when passing. 1: Player tosses ball, catches it at head level (hands spread in ten-point position), and then bounces it from stretched fingers. 2: Drop ball towards face of sitting player; return ball vertically.

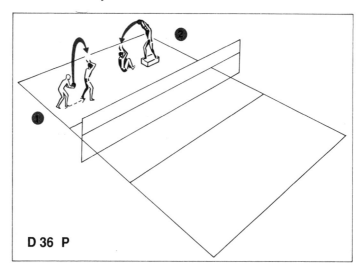

D 36   D 36 P

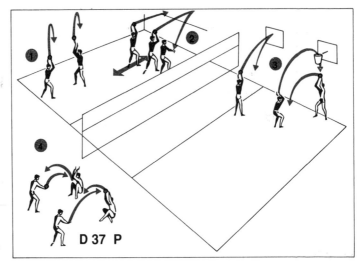

D 37

D 37 P

Preparatory passing drills. 1: Throw ball up into air, and then make an overhead pass to yourself. 2: Make passes against wall. 3: Pass the ball to a target. 4: Pass the ball to a sitting partner (hand/finger techniques and use of arms).

Preparatory passing drills. 1: Play the ball while moving forwards. 2: Play ball into the air and carry out additional tasks. 3: Pass ball against two walls. 4: Pass ball up into the air at different heights; 5: Play ball into the air, touch wall and carry out as a competition exercise.

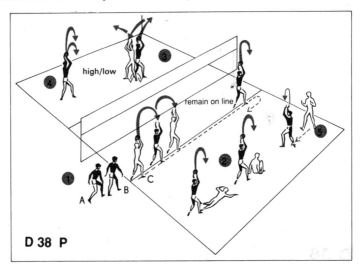

high/low

remain on line

A   B   C

D 38 P

D 38

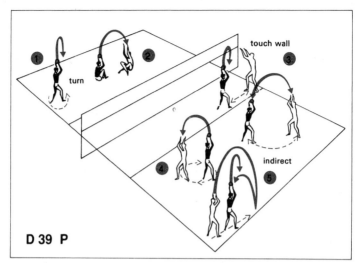

D 39 P

D 39

Passing under different conditions. 1: Pass, turn around underneath ball. 2: Pass in sitting positions. 3: Pass ball to yourself. 4: Walk in a circle and play ball up into air. 5: Indirect passing: bounce ball, crouch down, and volley.

Preparatory passing drills. 1: Bounce ball then pass. 2: Alternate between passing to yourself and against wall. 3: Play ball in zigzag fashion along wall. 4: Play ball off wall crouched down or in falling position. 5: Play ball up into air; turn, pass overhead, turn, etc.

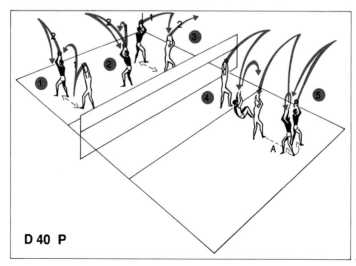

D 40 P

D 40

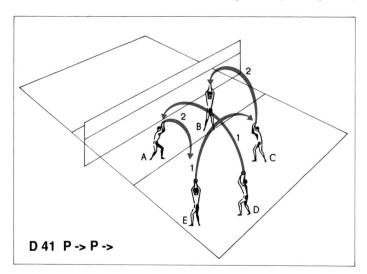

D 41 P -> P ->

D 41

In fives with two balls. Five players stand in a circle and pass to each other; this helps train peripheral vision (concentration focussed on pass being made directly and on preparation for next pass). When making your pass watch where the other ball is played.

Keeping several balls "In the air." Play balls vertically into the air and run quickly to the next ball. In position underneath ball, play up into air in front of head.

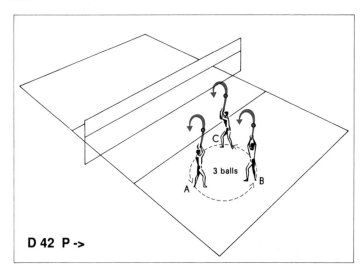

D 42 P ->

D 42

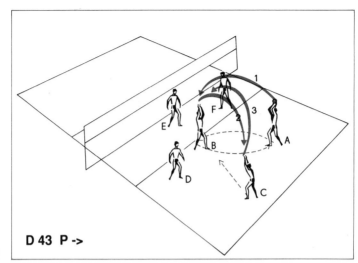

D 43

D 43 P ->

Change to centre of circle. Initially, play ball continuously to next player. Then, run to place where ball was played.

Pass in a triangle and run around a marker - pass. 1: While practising with intermediate play, run around a marker; practise adopting correct playing position. 2: A passes to B, who passes to self, turns, and passes back to C.

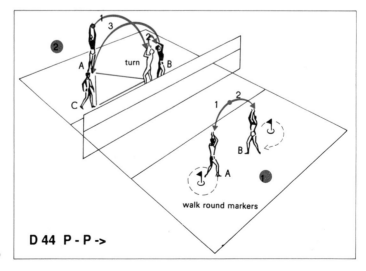

D 44

D 44 P - P ->

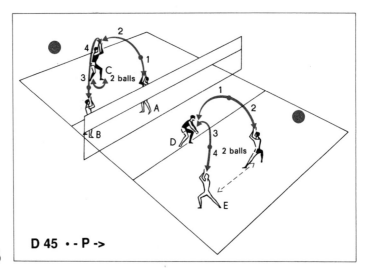

D 45

Pass after turning on spot and running sideways towards ball. 1:
Practise with two balls. 2: Throw balls in different directions; move quickly
right and left, return balls correctly.

**Alternation between volley and bump passes on court with two
balls and different playing directions**. Perform various movement sequences; decide which to use depending upon flight path of ball. Turn
completely towards direction of play (B bumps to A, volleys to C).

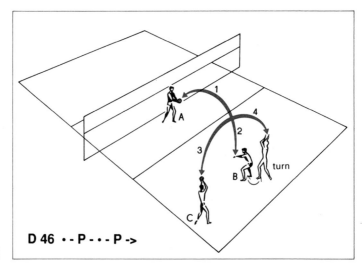

D 46 · - P - · - P ->

D 46

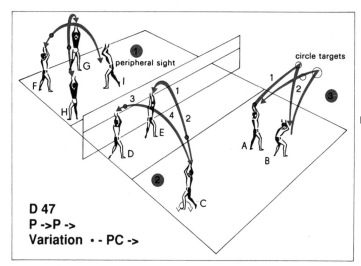

D 47

D 47
P ->P ->
Variation • - PC ->

Passes with several balls. 1: Balls are crossed. 2: After turning on spot alternate plays to players D-and E. 3: Overhead pass to partner via marked wall target.

Different passes under simplified conditions. 1: Jump pass with intermediate play (play ball to medium height). 2: In lateral falling position. 3: Falling backwards (crouch down when running forwards, go "underneath" ball).

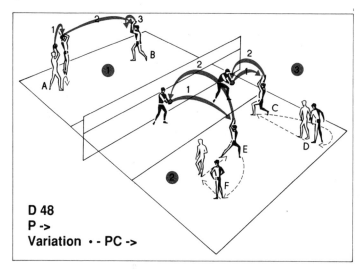

D 48

D 48
P ->
Variation • - PC ->

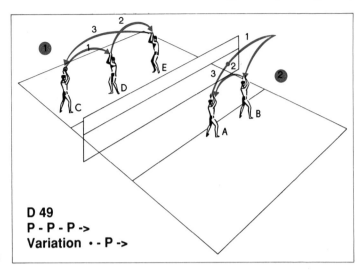

D 49
P - P - P ->
Variation • - P ->

D 49

Back pass after rebound from wall or pass from partner. 1: Centre player passes back. 2: Partner tosses ball against wall (target circle); pass rebounds back.

Passing balls in three on line. Concentrate on movement execution and passing accuracy to partner. Who can complete the most rounds? Practise at net or at least on a line.

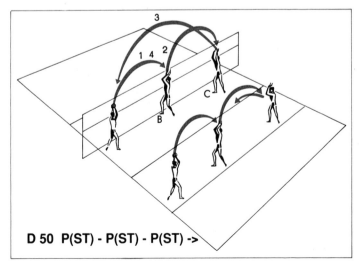

D 50 P(ST) - P(ST) - P(ST) ->

D 50

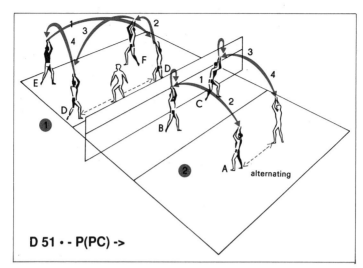

D 51 • - P(PC) ->

D 51

After moving sideways pass with and without changes in direction.
1: Pass ball diagonally, run to right and left, volley. 2: Passes on court
using in alternation players B and C; these players may also pass to
themselves.

Change position after each pass. 1: After passing to H, player I runs
through middle, receives the ball from H and plays to G, etc. 2: Players
from two groups take turns running up to net and passing.

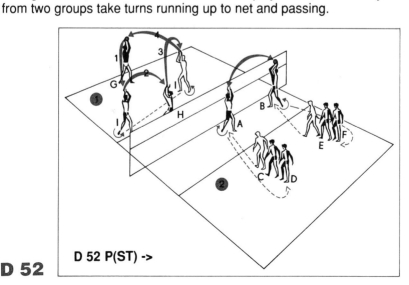

D 52 P(ST) ->

D 52

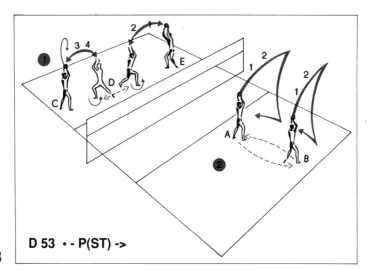

D 53   D 53 • - P(ST) ->

Combine volley with speed requirements. 1: Take turns playing to
players E and C. Control drill with passes to yourself if necessary. 2: A
and B play against wall and change positions after each pass, etc.

Keep ball constantly in the air at one position. 1: Take turns running
underneath the ball and playing it high in the air. 2: After playing the ball
into air run quickly towards the wall. Increase speed requirements by decreasing height of pass.

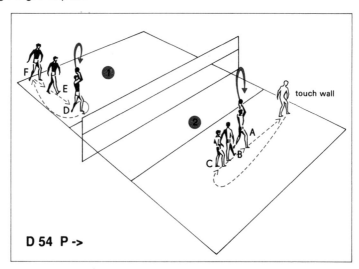

D 54   D 54 P ->

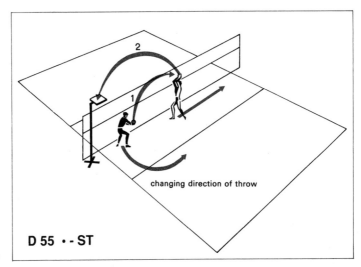

changing direction of throw

D 55 · - ST

D 55

Setting to target basket. Work through movement sequence first under simplified conditions; increase distance and direction for throwing ball to player. Concentrate on main points in the sequence.

Setting to target basket as back-row setter. Do not begin moving until ball is thrown. Remain stationary first (right shoulder facing net), then play. Concentrate on execution of the movement (use entire body).

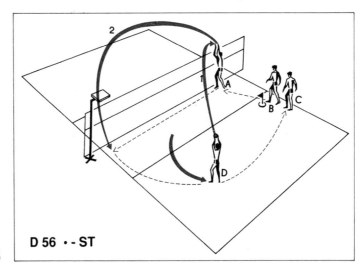

D 56 · - ST

D 56

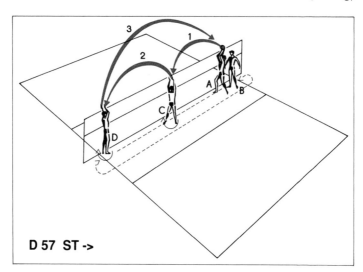

D 57 ST ->

D 57

Back and forward setting. Movement sequence becomes fixed with continuous practice. Assume position quickly and play correctly. How many sequences can you complete without interruption? A passes to C, runs to position D; C back passes to D, runs to position B (B becomes A); D-passes to B, runs to position A.

Setting over greater distance and following ball (shuttle movement). Play high, direct passes to court side lines and do not come too close to the net. Make sure to use entire body.

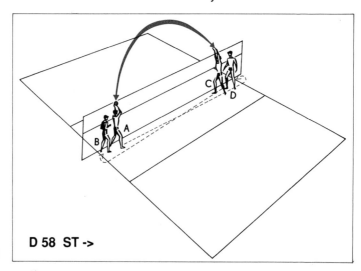

D 58 ST ->

D 58

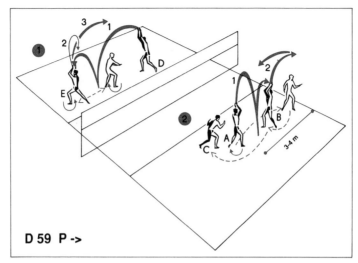

D 59

D 59 P ->

Pass back. 1: Play back pass up into air. Turn and make overhead pass to player D; D-passes, lets ball bounce; E plays back pass up in air, etc. 2: A bounce passes to B, who back passes against wall; A runs quickly to wall and awaits pass from C.

After ball bounces take turns playing against wall. Combine moving quickly towards ball and running around marker with accurate volley (hit target circle on wall).

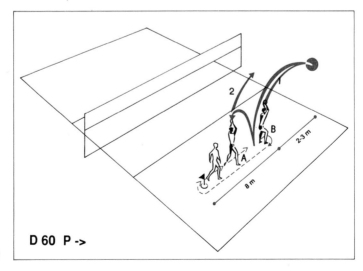

D 60

D 60 P ->

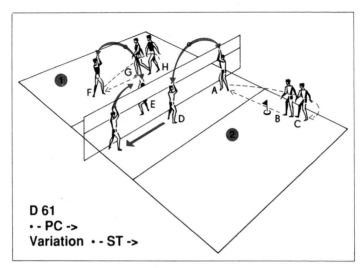

D 61
• - PC ->
Variation • - ST ->

D 61

Lateral approach and pass. 1: Keep alternating between lateral approach and passes on court. 2: Prepare to set as back-row setter; delay starting until ball is played; approach quickly, turn, and make a standing pass while standing still.

Set several times in a row. Coach plays ball; players change position for passing accordingly and use different passes (if closer to position 2, long pass to position 4; if closer to position 3, back to position 2).

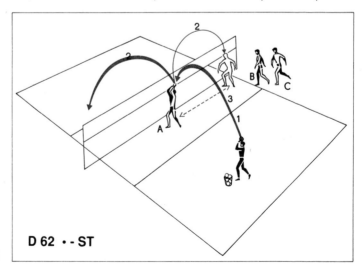

D 62 • - ST

D 62

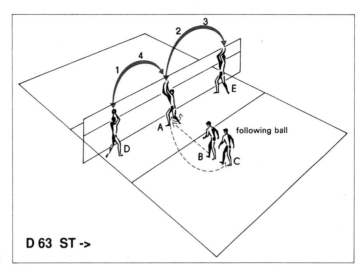

D 63

D 63 ST ->

Setting in threes parallel to net. Centre player begins by changing only after two passes (to D-and E); later after each pass. Make sure you complete one full turn into direction of play.

Run quickly around a marker and pass. Preparation for setting as back-row setter. After each play run around marker. Variation: two players practise on each side; do not move away from marker until opposite partner makes pass.

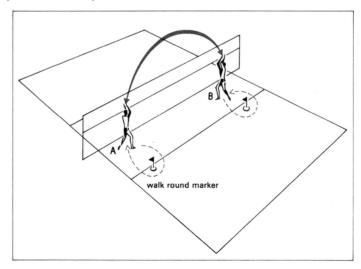

walk round marker

D 64

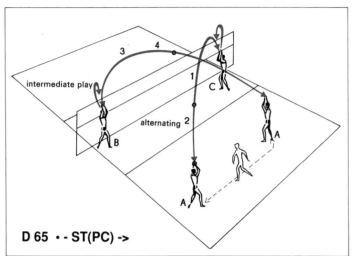

D 65 ·-ST(PC) ->

D 65

Run quickly right and left and pass diagonally. Take turns playing diagonally to positions 2 and 4. Run quickly right and left, turn towards direction of intended pass and make pass in standing-still position (note arms and footwork). Combine movement towards ball with pass over greater distance. (B and C may pass to themselves to control the drill better.)

Pass diagonally after ball played by coach. A plays ball to coach, who then returns ball to neighbouring position. A moves quickly to this position and makes high pass to position 3. Vary basic and passing positions.

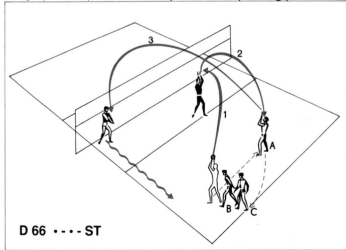

D 66 ····-ST

D 66

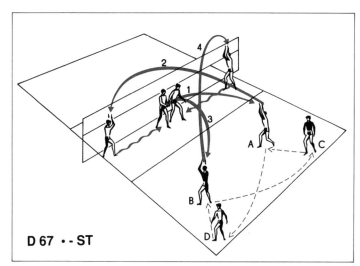

D 67 • - ST

D 67

Alternate continuously between positions 1 and 5. After each diagonal pass (or bump) change to next position. Auxiliary player must ensure supply of balls.

Practise diagonal passes individually. Bounce ball, run under it and pass up to position 2 or 4; vary starting position on court. Make sure to use entire body. Concentrate on accuracy of movement sequence and target accuracy when working at low pace.

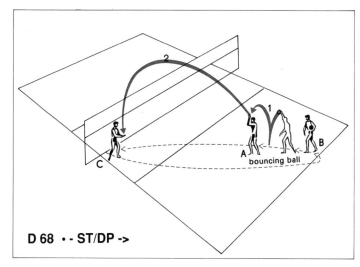

bouncing ball

D 68 • - ST/DP ->

D 68

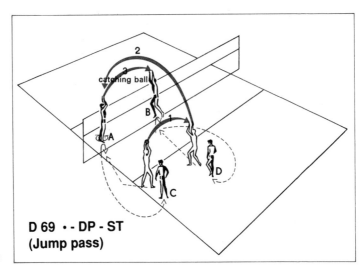

D 69

D 69 • - DP - ST
(Jump pass)

Direct pass to position 4 - jump pass. After ball is played A assumes offensive position; B passes diagonally to position 4; A makes medium high jump pass to position 3, where player B is in attack formation. For player A, approach as in attack, take off, swing arm back; then turn and pass. Make attacks tactical.

Direct passes after easy ball from opponent. Do not play to player but to empty part of court instead. Run quickly to playing position and set direct passes to position 4. Variation: with difficult balls, use bump passes.

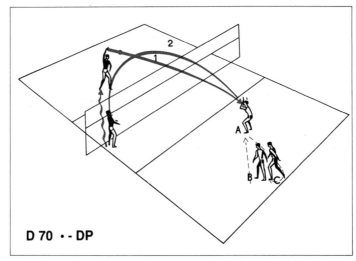

D 70 • - DP

D 70

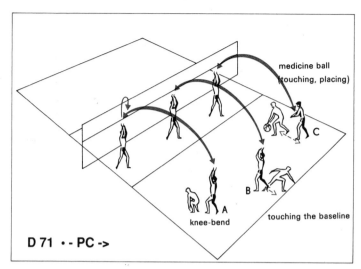

D 71

Passes on court with other tasks. Partner passes ball to himself or herself; ball is then played immediately directly to A who returns pass; A watches partner while completing other task.

Passing on court and chasing after ball. Practise vertically (F and G) or diagonally (A and C) to net. Depending upon ball played from net, volley or bump the ball. Count out loud. Which group can make the most passes on court without interruption?

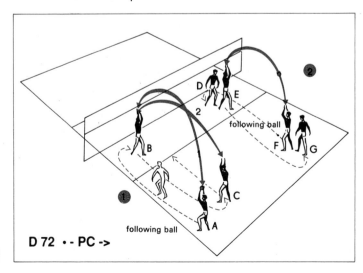

D 72

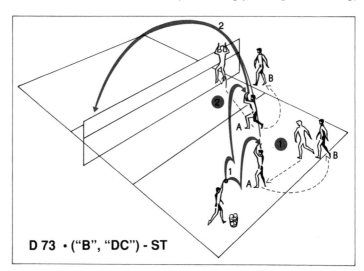

D 73

D 73 • ("B", "DC") - ST

Diagonal passes after previous plays. Coach bounces ball; A plays accurate high diagonal passes to position 4; then A goes and performs secondary activities like block jump; steady drill pace with numerous repetitions.

Setting and covering attacker in pairs. A plays ball to position 2; C sets to position 4 (close to net). A and C, after ball is played, go immediately to attack coverage and recover simulated block rebound.

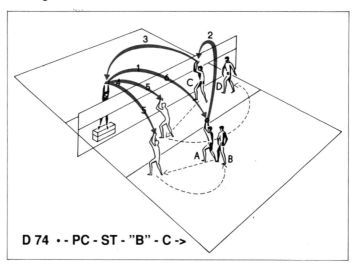

D 74

D 74 • - PC - ST - "B" - C ->

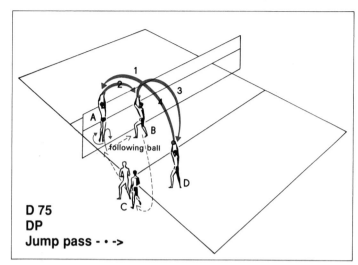

D 75

D 75
DP
Jump pass - • ->

Jump pass as direct pass after ball is played. Concentrate only on jump pass at first, then vary actions (good direct pass should engage jump pass, poor direct pass an immediate attack). Jump first, then turn. D-passes to A; A jump passes to B; B back passes to D, etc.

Play different balls after forward and sideways movement. 1: Run forwards, pass on court, return immediately, etc. 2: Change position constantly while moving sideways: practise continuously, 15 to 20 times.

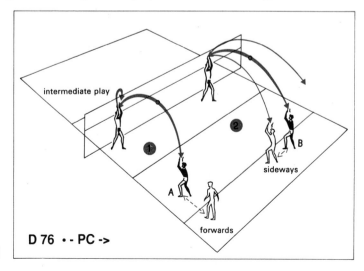

D 76

D 76 • - PC ->

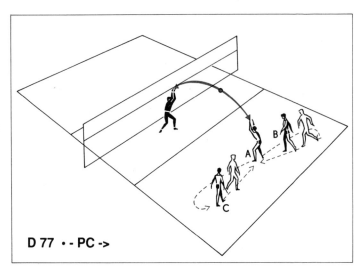

D 77 · - PC ->

D 77

Approach from right and left - pass on court. Coach always plays to position 6. Players approach from right and left and play directly back to coach. Bump or volley ball depending upon ball trajectory.

Pass on court over greater distance. Coach plays ball (hits, volleys); player A bumps or volleys ball to C, who sets ball to coach. With increased skill, C can set ball more quickly and in a flatter way so as to prepare for offensive combinations.

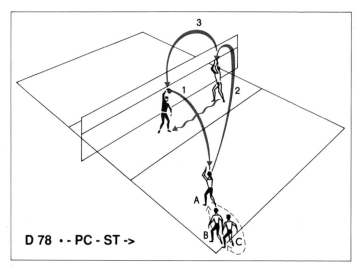

D 78 · - PC - ST ->

D 78

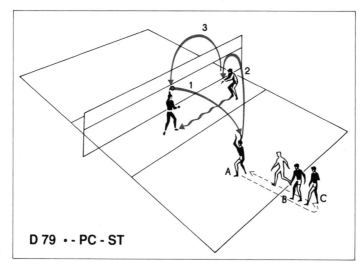

D 79

D 79 · - PC - ST

Bump or volley with change in direction. Remain stationary before contacting ball. Aim for maximum accuracy. Coach varies height of flight path of ball when playing.

Passes on court moving back and forward/passes on court back to coach. 1: Players volley or bump ball. When partner has ball in hands, move forwards; after pass return immediately. 2: Pass on court with hitting or throwing balls of varying difficulty.

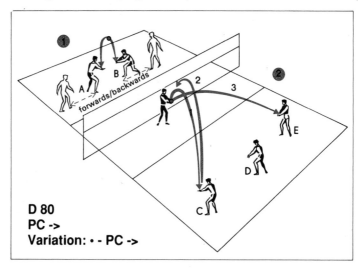

D 80

D 80
PC ->
Variation: · - PC ->

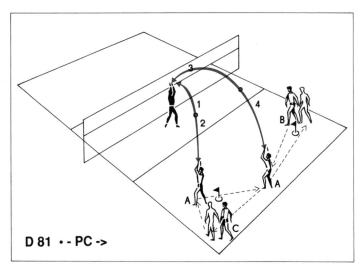

D 81 · - PC ->

D 81

Two passes on court after moving from different directions. A runs forwards towards the ball, makes pass on court back to coach. (After moving sideways to position 6 A plays another court pass.) Then A goes to behind B. Coach starts sequence with B.

Predicting direction of initial ball - pass on court . Coach plays ball irregularly. Ready to act, you should observe coach's actions carefully. Run quickly to where the ball is thrown and, as situation dictates, make correct passes on court.

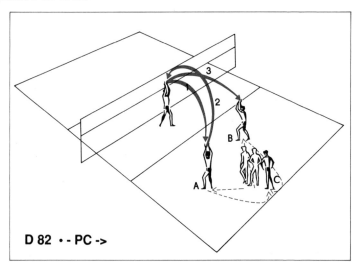

D 82 · - PC ->

D 82

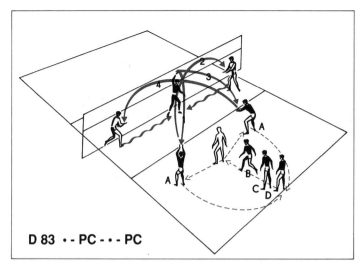

D 83   D 83 • - PC - • - PC

After variable initial balls make passes on court right and left .
Complete two successive passes on court. Player begins at centre court,
turns towards direction of ball from coach and makes diagonal pass. In
the case of flat balls use sidearm bump.
Passes on court with changes in passing direction. Player at net
changes position shortly before pass. This drill trains peripheral vision.
Initially throw ball accurately, aiming at a specific player, then throw ball
variably.

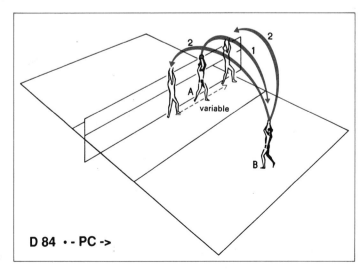

D 84   D 84 • - PC ->

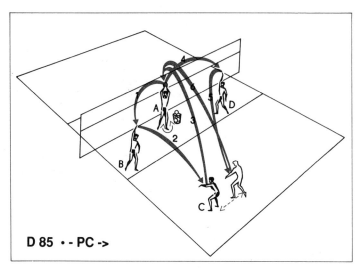

D 85 · - PC ->

D 85

Non-stop passes on court with two balls. Play from different directions; bump ball. Maximum concentration is needed to master play. Begin using one ball. Increase difficulty by changing initial passes by players B and D (i.e.,volley, easy spike, hard spike).

Two successive passes on court. Balls thrown variably from position 5 (feint, block rebound) must be played accurately to the net. Decide which technique, overhead or bump pass is the best.

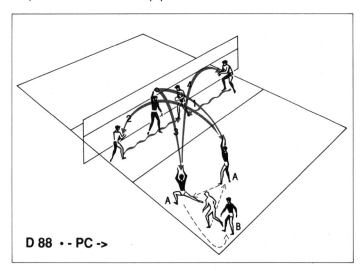

D 88 · - PC ->

D 86

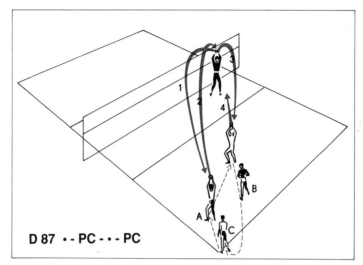

D 87 · - PC - · - PC

D 87

Return ball directly to coach twice. Practise at varying distances from point where ball was initially thrown. Accuracy calls for quick changes in execution of plays.

Passes on court in different directions after variable initial balls. Balls are played and passed on court at random; accurate play is essential. Improve variations for passing on court with numerous repetitions.

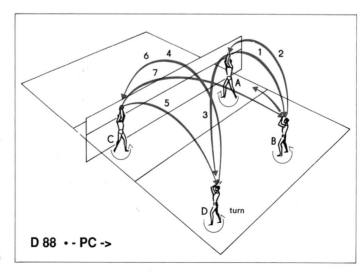

D 88 · - PC ->

D 88

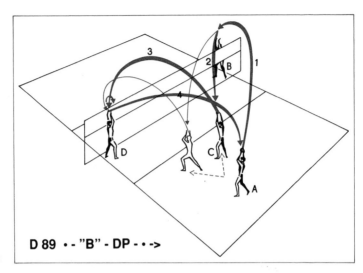

D 89   D 89 · - "B" - DP - · ->

Direct passes after variable initial balls. A passes to B who simulates tip or high block rebounds - C court passes as direct pass to position 4. Play balls simply at first, then increase difficulty. Use variations for passing such as in falling or rolling position.

Turning towards direction of play when setting parallel to net.
Player A plays ball with back to net (1). Player B bumps or volleys pass on court (2). Player A turns towards direction of play and passes to self (3), turns and begins again. Change after 10 times.

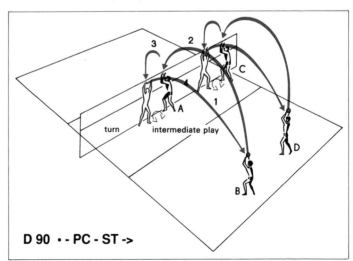

D 90   D 90 · - PC - ST ->

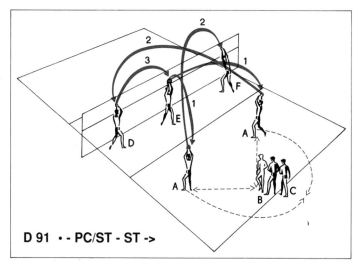

D 91 • - PC/ST - ST ->

D 91

Pass on court after moving right or left. The ball is played either right or left. From ready start position, run quickly to starting position; turn around behind ball, remain stationary and make pass on court. Pass on court to players D or F.

Non-stop direct passes. Run forwards from position 1 to the front line and play thrown ball as a first pass to position 4. (simulate feint or block rebound).

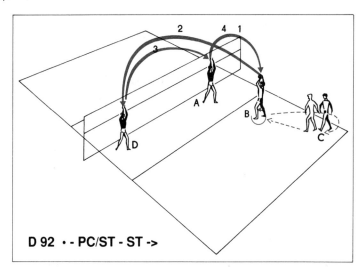

D 92 • - PC/ST - ST ->

D 92

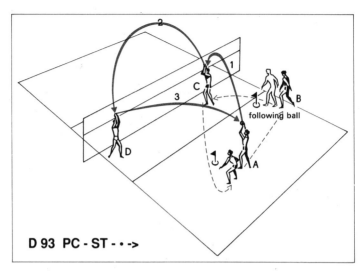

D 93

D 93 PC - ST - • ->

After pass on court make high passes as back-row setter. Practise continuously to improve high passes to position 4. Volley accurately from centre court. Player D varies first ball more and more.

Pass on court or direct passes alternating between positions 2 and 4. Assume playing position quickly and return balls directly to positions 2 and 4: or play in such a way that a direct pass attack is possible. Vary initial balls. H receives jump pass from G or F and passes to A, who passes to C, who in turn sets positions 2 and 4.

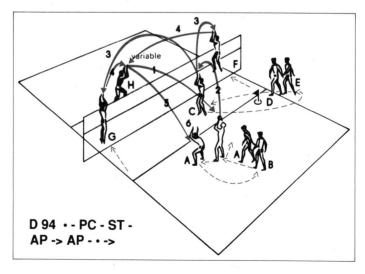

D 94 • - PC - ST -
AP -> AP - • ->

D 94

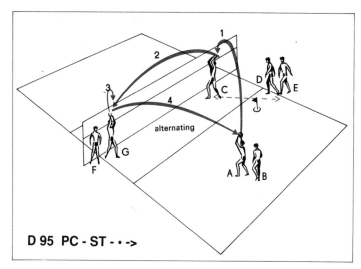

D 95 PC - ST - • ->

D 95

After pass on court play flat, rapid passes. Practise continuously as in D 96. "Push" passes on court somewhat flatter and more quickly forwards. Practise setting and jumping as well.

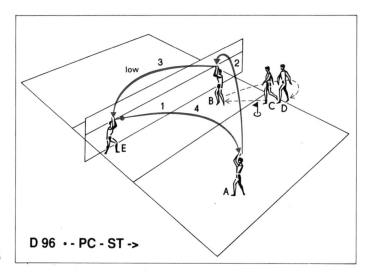

D 96 • - PC - ST ->

D 96

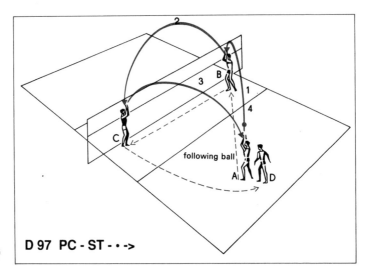

D 97

D 97 PC - ST - • ->

Passes on court - non-stop high passes. Continuous exercising as in
D 95 and 96; as fixed frontcourt passer set to position 4. Volley or bump
pass depending upon distance from passer.

Setting to position 4 after simulation of bump in centre of court.
Change playing position of fixed frontcourt passer in relation to passes
on court. Remember complete turn toward direction of passing.

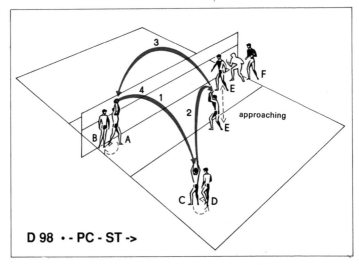

D 98

D 98 • - PC - ST ->

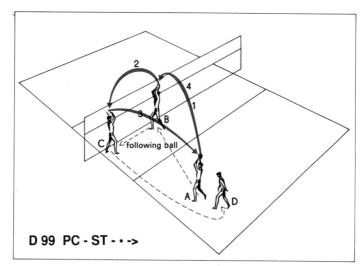

D 99

D 99 PC - ST - • ->

Setting over short distance. Combine pass on court with setting in simple forms. Pay close attention during passes on court - high and not too close to net. Continuous drill - follow the pass.

Combination court pass - setting. Player A plays ball to empty area of court. Backcourt players penetrate to position 4 and play directly to fixed passer at position 3.

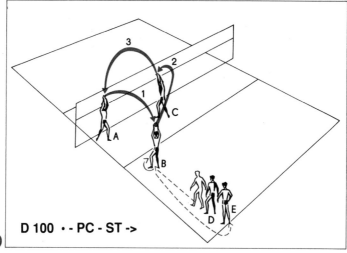

D 100

D 100 • - PC - ST ->

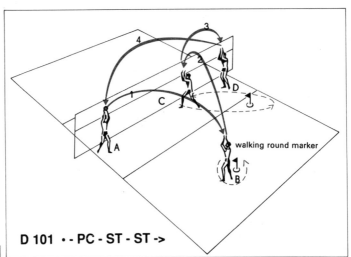

D 101 · · - PC - ST - ST ->

D 101

Pass on court - back pass - high pass to position 4. Practise
continuously. Player B and C run around marker before each pass. Back-
row setter (C) makes back pass; fixed passer D-makes high pass to
position 4.
Diagonal (direct) passes alternating between positions 2 and 4.
Practise continuously with diagonal passes after easy passes from
positions 2 and 4. Starting direction and passing direction are not the
same. Run - stand still - play.

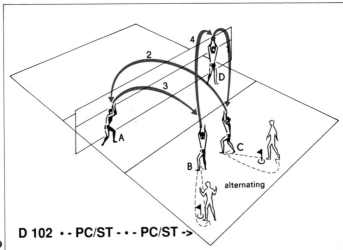

D 102 · · - PC/ST - · · · - PC/ST ->

D 102

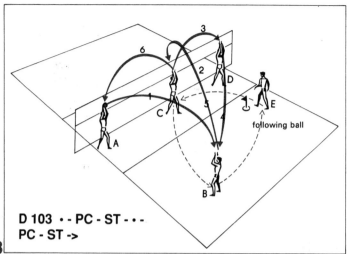

D 103 · - PC - ST - · · -
PC - ST ->

D 103

Variable setting by back-row setter after pass on court. Passing position is between positions 2 and 3. Pass on court goes more towards position 3 - back pass, court pass more towards position 2 - "long" pass to position 4. Practise continuously.

Forward and back setting after pass on court from different directions. Prepare for variable initial balls; change passing position. Increase requirements for passing on court gradually.

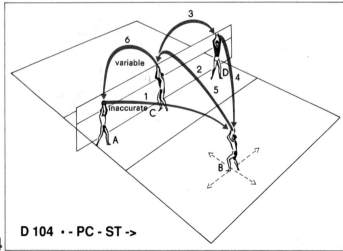

D 104 · - PC - ST ->

D 104

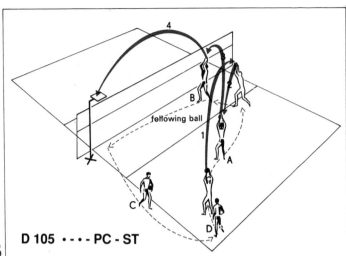

D 105

D 105 · · · - PC - ST

Combine pass on court with setting to target. Passes on court over short distance. Move to playing position and set accurately to position 4. Steady drill pace with time for corrections.

Back set with changes in passing position. Indirect initial ball; "feeling" for correct playing position and precise execution of movement without seeing ball being thrown are required. Player B always begins between positions 2 and 3.

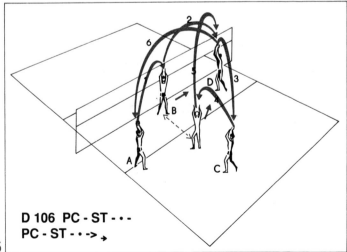

D 106 PC - ST - · · -
PC - ST - · ·-> ,

D 106

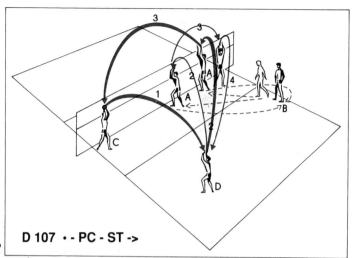

D 107

D 107 · - PC - ST ->

Pass on court combined with different variations for setting. Irregular passes on court towards positions 2 or 3. Passers decide whether they make normal play (to position 4) or back set. Ball close to position 3 - back pass; ball outside (close to position 2) - play it long and forward to position 4.

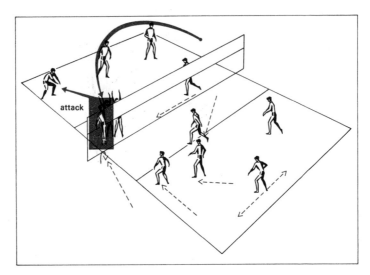

3.4   The Attack

3.4.1   General characteristics

To win the game each side tries to conclude its own series of plays with a powerful spike. The importance of the spike is explained by the fact that all preceding plays are necessary in preparing for the attack, but the success or failure in offence is in the end critical for the effectiveness of the entire series of actions.

Well driven spikes are a very dynamic and significant component of the game. The wealth of variations used in preparation for and in execution of the spike, the combination of elegant sequences with explosive energy (jumps, quick setting), as well the finesse observable in the offensive plays, spur players and spectators alike. Although spiking is the main method used to win the game, from the point of view of training methodology, however, coaches must try not to overemphasize this element. The ability to attack is not synonymous with playing volleyball. A team of "only-attackers" will not be able over the long run to play the game successfully.

The effectiveness of an attack is defined by a variety of factors. There is hardly any other play element that displays the entire complexity of volleyball play actions. Players need to be able to master a number of variations for spiking performance. They cannot perform the spike unless they have excellent *athletic abilities*. Without well-developed athletic skills (speed, explosive power for jumps, jumping, and power endurance, etc.) the spike cannot be properly executed. *Cognitive* qualities (perception, mental assessment of game situations, motor decisions), including tactical knowledge and previous experience, are also essential for successful attack action. Finally, *mental* and *psychological performance* (self-confidence, psychological stamina, sense of responsibility, etc.) play a major role.

When all of these factors become more developed and teams use more group tactical offensive plays (offensive combinations), the chances of successful attack increase. The more offensive variations players know, the more possibilities they have to resolve situation-governed game tasks. Winning or losing game initiative is therefore determined primarily by improving offensive play.

Offensive styles are very numerous, making it difficult to elaborate a clear and complete classification. This difficulty is compounded by variations in the main characteristics of player movement, fluid transitions between the variations for attacking and, lastly, transitional forms. Nowhere is the wide range of offensive possibilities more visible than in the variations in hitting power and direction. When the entire width of the net is used, players attack from not only frontcourt positions (2, 3, 4) but also from intermediate positions. Successful teams now also attack from the "second line" (backcourt). Innumerable variations in the repertory for offensive techniques and tactics result from different spiking power, movement of arms in relation to the position of shoulder axis, changes in shoulder axis when hitting, and the many possible combinations for offence and passing.

Despite all these variations, we conclude, however, that the *fundamental motor movement* characteristics involved can be standardized. These include the individual stages during the approach, planting the feet, taking off, swinging the arms, the maximum height of arm action, and the landing. A specific, basic repertory of attacking will include the following variations: *jump set* (beginners), *running spike* (smash, lob), *tips* (tip and power tip), *wrist shot* variations (hitting block), *spike with turn of body* and *spike from quick sets*. Other methods used mostly by specialists are *the screen* or *across the body spike* and the *roundhouse or hook spike*.

3.4.2 Teaching the Spike

In keeping with our intention to proceed as quickly as possible to play under actual conditions, the attack should have been learned before the actual spike is mastered. As a variation of overhead passing we have learned the *stationary* and *jump set pass*, which is relatively easy to use later in play as a one-hand tip or lob. Learning the overhead serve is at the same time a methodical step towards learning the spike; one-handed shots for serving can also be used as an initial variation for practising the spike within the court. In the next stage of training, players must learn to practise spiking from high ball passes, followed by attacking using quick, attack sets until they can combine each of these different variations and are able to use them. A mastery of simple variations for setting is essential to successful spiking. Spatial and temporal co-ordination in simple types of games, the execution of plays as they are done in the game and overall movement on the court are an important preparatory step. Even without the spike, players can systematically practise offensive formation and its variations (different offensive systems).

The complexity of the movement sequences and difficult co-ordination with a moving ball make it necessary to learn the attack gradually by breaking down the attack and *learning its component parts*. When learning the serve, in completing individual drills against a wall or exercising with a partner players, make stationary shots initially and concentrate on the swinging motion of the arm and the actual shot. This should be followed by practising the approach and take-off without the ball (with and without the net) and combining these drills with jump shots (tennis ball, rounders ball) over the net (swinging the arm back, hitting, two-foot landing). An important methodical step is *hitting a stationary ball*. Players can concentrate on the entire offensive play because the ball is at the same correct height and distance from the net regardless of the timing factor. When practising the approach, orientation aids (visual and acoustic) can also be used. Changing the height of the net also helps. When the net is low, players should practise only the standing spike (select net height so that players must make contact with the ball with arms extended). If allowed to spike normally players are inclined to drive powerful spikes, quickly resulting in the chief fault, the "bent arm." When the net is higher, *off speeds* and *tips* can also be practised. Whichever styles players adopt, they should try to develop an attacking capability that prevents the opposing team from digging or blocking the attack.

Finally, markers that guide players' movements and make possible an immediate comparison of planned actions and results, are to be recommended.

3.4.3   Coaching Tips

We have already said that players and coaches all too often concentrate exclusively on spiking. This misplaced emphasis is compounded by the erroneous assumption that a successful spike depends only on the power used. Often in training, players try to smash each ball, rarely practising placing the hit with less power into different areas of their opponents' court. This makes for ineffective results. Coaches therefore should ensure that when feeding the ball players use different types of shots and aim at specific targets. Once these skills have been learned adequately, players can proceed to offensive training primarily using complex drills that closely simulate near-game situations. Attackers must then match their actions with various game situations and must make tactical decisions. They will quickly notice that it is better to attack carefully and safely than running up and smashing the ball indiscriminately.

The main principle in training is to use the block in all offensive drills. In practising spiking within the game phases, players learn how to orient themselves properly in the game, to make decisions relevant to the situation, and to execute actions in conjunction with preceding and following plays.

Offensive training should be combined with practising the standard situations (service reception, defence, passing on court). Attackers must learn to perform these actions themselves and then move quickly to the attack; the accuracy with which they perform these standard situations determines the possibilities available for setting. Other near-game combinations are: block/attack, attack/defence (including block coverage) or attack/attack (with less preparation time).

Team play between setter and attacker is naturally very important for successful offensive training. Coaches must ensure from the beginning that players do not set automatically from the same position but adapt to changing setting positions, directions, variations in flight path and speed of ball.

For co-ordination in team play it is also important that the attacker does not always throw the ball while performing simple drills.

These drill combinations should make it possible to practise other technical and tactical plays at the same time as the attack without losing time for offensive training.

Rare offensive variations such as *attack from backcourt* or a *direct spike from an overset ball* are almost never trained in special drills but are rather scattered surprisingly throughout the drills by throwing in balls under the training aspect of matching technical execution with the situation. It is wise before proceeding, to practise these basic situations several times in isolation.

Essential to successful offensive combinations is co-ordinated team play (court awareness and timing) between setters and attackers. It cannot be assumed, then, that different combinations will immediately be successful in competition. Offensive combinations require a great deal of practice until they are suitable for competition, and must be developed gradually. Practise spiking at first together with special types of setting (short, quick to position 4 or short sets, at medium height to position 2, etc.). Different types of attacks can then be combined with these special sets until the entire front row attackers are included. It is imperative that blocking be included at this stage.

While good setting is important for beginners, experienced players must also be able to use poor sets to attack, at least without any direct faults. For this reason, in training attackers should not catch the ball if set poorly but rather attack even under these difficult conditions.

3.4.4   Tactical Rules

- Concern yourself primarily with attacking efficiently and sensibly. Do not play at utmost force for the sake of success and above all, avoid obvious errors.
- Watch other players as they perform the actions on which you have to base your performance (defending serve, court defence, court passes.) Make every attempt to identify possibilities for the set by considering flight path of the set and the setter's movements. Co-ordinate your offensive play exactly with the setter and watch the opponents' block when making your decisions.
- Try to attack successfully even with poor sets. Use good sets responsibly and do not use poor sets as an excuse for offensive errors.
- Hit shots to uncovered areas of the court or to weak defensive players. Before attacking have an idea about the opponents' defensive formation and the ability of individual players.
- Assume a ready position opportunely at the attack line (move rapidly away from the net or away from the defensive position).
- Run towards the net diagonally if possible, and do not begin the approach on a high set until the ball has left the setter's hands (for "metre" balls, the final plant is made when the ball is set; with "short sets", the approach and plant occur before the set).
- Choose a take-off spot so that you are able to hit the ball in front of your body. Make a powerful jump and try to hit the ball at maximum possible height.
- Vary offensive play, taking into consideration the opponents' block and defence. Frequently change the direction in which you hit, also vary the strength with which you strike the ball and use different types of attack, as the opponents tend to settle quickly for routine attacks. Experienced

players actively practise varying approach angles—especially in association with specific combinations.

- Hard shots immediately beyond the net are advisable only without a block or with a mistimed block.
- With a good two-player block, use the blocker's hands, off speeds, or tips behind the block, or hit wrist shots in front of or over block. Try to push balls close to the net into the block or "roll" a hard-driven spike up and off the block.
- Alternate between making long power spikes to backcourt and placing the hit (off-speed or tip) to the frontcourt. Successful off speeds or tips to the frontcourt can be made especially effective after several successfully dug spikes.
- Direct your attacks to the back court if the opposing defence orientates too much to the front court.
- After an outside set, hit down the line as much as possible. With sets far inside, approach and hit diagonally (cross-court) or tip if facing a well-formed block.
- Be careful with balls coming high from the opponents' court. The flight path is different than when setting, and the ball often descends faster.

3.4.5   Drill Pool

Preparatory drills (learning the spike): D 108 to D 113.
Offensive sets: D 114 to D 123.
Spiking (after the set, specific types of attack): D 124 to D 136.

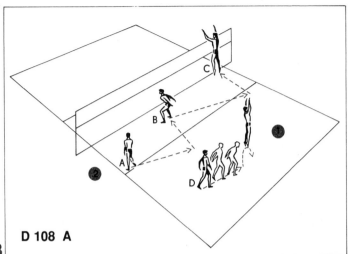

D 108 A

D 108

Learning the spike (preparatory drills). 1: Experiment with approach rhythm and take-off (take-off position identical to landing position); 2: Practise planting the feet aggressively. 3: Plant your right foot and pivot on it, put left leg in front sideways, with the foot turned slightly inwards.

Learning the spike (preparatory drills). 1: Approach, jump up at basketball basket. 2: Jump and throw the ball over net. 3: Smash the ball indirectly against wall (stand erect when hitting; cupping hands around ball).

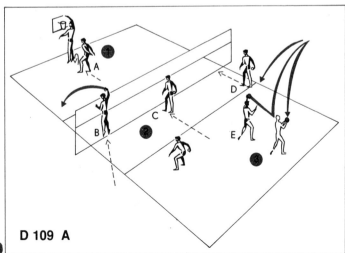

D 109 A

D 109

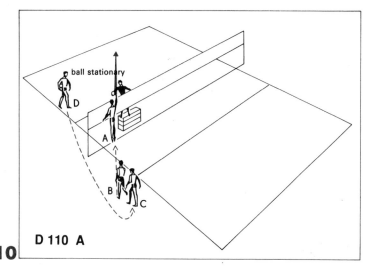

D 110 A

D 110

Spiking with stationary ball. Coach or a player holds the ball at the correct height and distance from the net; attacker can concentrate on spiking without having to consider flight path.

Spiking after balls thrown. Balls are thrown to player at medium height; simplify co-ordination of the approach with flight path of ball.

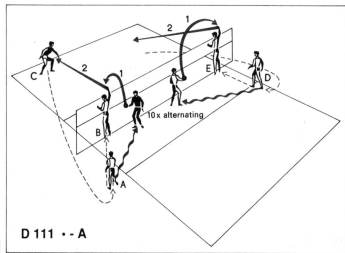

D 111 · - A

D 111

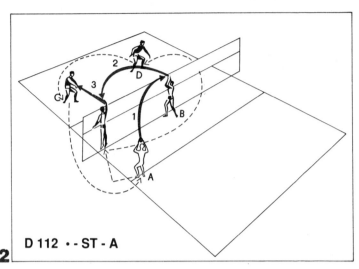

D 112 · - ST - A

D 112

Spike after tossing ball to setter. Concentrate on completing one action first, then proceed with the next one. Wait for set, then approach quickly. Practise this exercise from all offensive positions.

Spike after ball tossed by coach. Several players take turns hitting the ball; attackers can concentrate completely on approach and hitting of the spike.

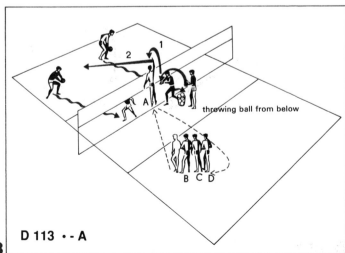

throwing ball from below

D 113 · - A

D 113

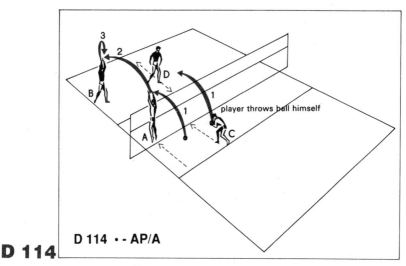

player throws ball himself

D 114 · - AP/A

D 114

Toss ball to yourself - offensive pass. Learning offensive jump pass. Watch partner when practising and play directly to him with a two-handed pass. Variation: defensive player changes position when taking off.

Toss ball to yourself in stationary or jump shots. Learn the correct position in relation to ball and hitting motion, while standing and as you jump. Use off speeds. (Do not follow through with arm after hitting the ball.)

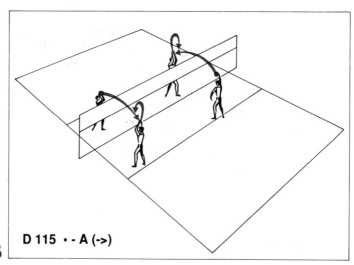

D 115 · - A (->)

D 115

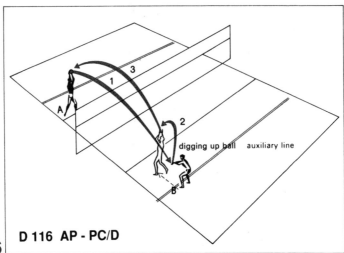

D 116   D 116   AP - PC/D

Passing over net to partner with intermediate pass. Practise at short distances at first and receive ball with overhead pass. Pass to self. Then increase distance and recover with bump. (Receive each pass from A, pass to self, approach and volley back to A.)

After intermediate pass spike to moving and fixed targets. 1: Learn different strength required by changing distance from net. 2: Make offensive passes to target (alternate between short/long). Score. (Easy pass from A to B, B passes to self, volleys to either different spots on floor or partner who changes position.)

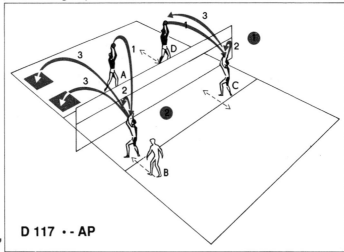

D 117   D 117   · - AP

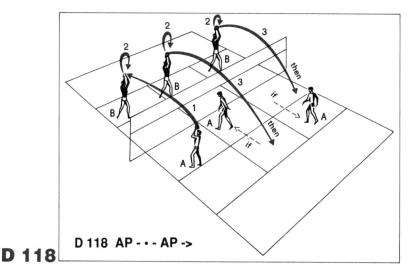

D 118 AP - • - AP ->

D 118

Attack passes "1 on 1". Return ball after a minimum of one pass to self. Offensive passes to empty areas of court. Match: timed play or up to 10 points; normal tallying method and change of serves.

Offensive passes to empty court. Play the ball to an empty part of court, depending upon actions by both opponents. The latter run for the ball and return it or assume tasks of A and B.

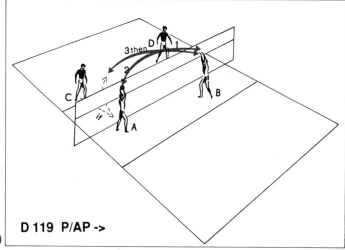

D 119 P/AP ->

D 119

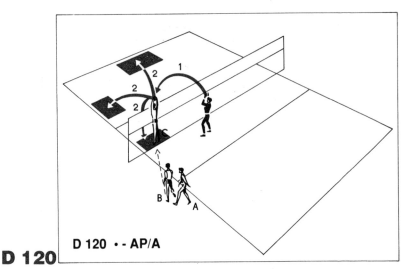

D 120

D 120 · - AP/A

Offensive jump sets to fixed targets. The ball thrown from position 3 (use the same approach as when spiking); use offensive pass (announce actions beforehand or fix target depending upon how ball is thrown).

Offensive jump passes with two defensive players. Player A plays to position 4; attackers jump and spike the ball. Try to play to uncovered areas on court; defensive players should return the ball after one mandatory pass.

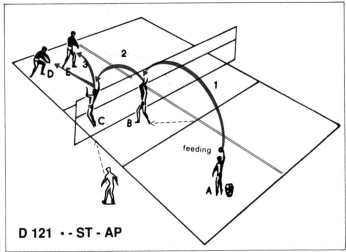

D 121

D 121 · - ST - AP

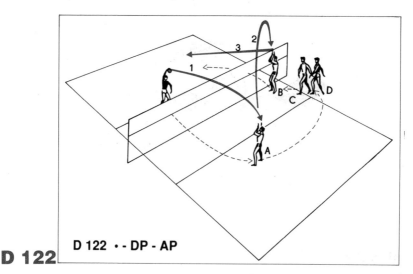

D 122

D 122 · - DP - AP

Passes on court (direct) for attack. Attack using easy ball from opponent - direct pass to position 2 - player B makes offensive jump-pass or spike over the net.

Offensive jump-passes after court pass and set . Ball is thrown from opponents' half (player A); C uses volley or bump passes; B sets across even greater distance; D-makes offensive jump passes directly to partner (player A), then to uncovered areas on court. Offspeeds and tips can be used later on as well.

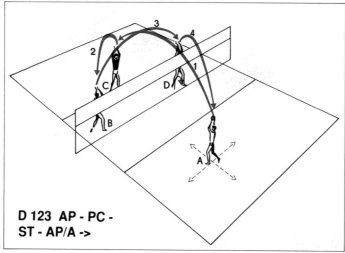

D 123 AP - PC -
ST - AP/A ->

D 123

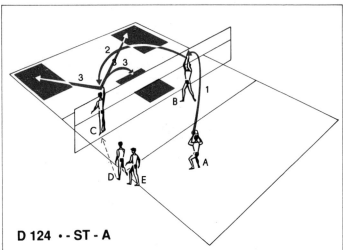

D 124

D 124 · - ST - A

Spiking to target. Compare between intended and achieved results; these are initial basis for improving players' motor skills. They should be able to determine how the movements are to be practised, or the amount of power required.

Attack in approach direction or with turn. High passes. Spike to target. Spike balls in centre of court in run-off direction and turn before you play "outward bound" passes. Variation: watch the block before you determine the direction in which you strike.

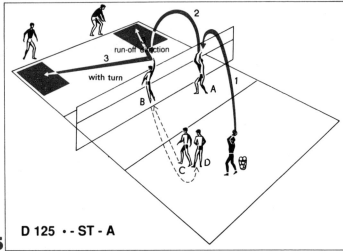

D 125

D 125 · - ST - A

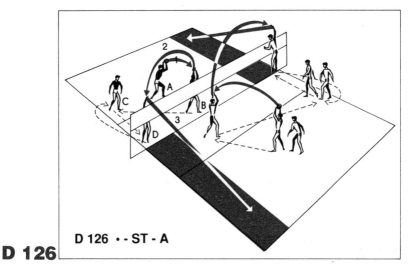

D 126

D 126 · - ST - A

Spike behind setter. Line attack from position 2 from medium and high passes. Getting accustomed to lack of optical control between setter and attacker. Approach from centre to outside and do not begin prematurely.

Spike with high passes down line. Player A alternates setting high passes to positions 2 and 4. Attackers change position after 5 to 10 times. Try to hit the ball at maximum possible height.

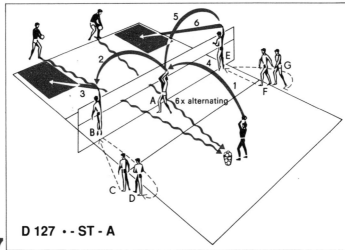

D 127

D 127 · - ST - A

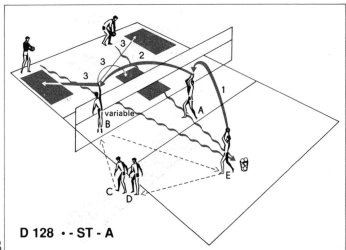

D 128

D 128 · - ST - A

Learning offensive combinations. Develop timing and co-ordination between setter and attacker for specific passes (use a long, flat pass to position 4). Attack should end with spike to target and include a single-player block.

Spike with high parallel passes past block. Use sets from greater distance. If block sets up outside - spike cross-court ; if block inside - spike down the line; balls close to net - spike in the block. Blockers change after 5 spikes.

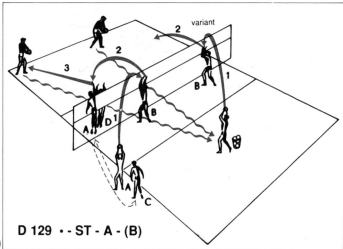

D 129

D 129 · - ST - A - (B)

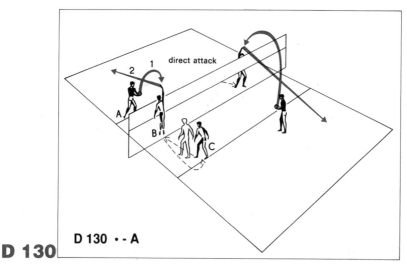

D 130

D 130 · - A

Direct spike after oversets from opponent. Throw ball to edge of net. Power spike (stationary) or powerful jump with a one-step approach and hitting arm extended. Do not try to overkill (smash trap).

Direct spike with oversets from opponent. 1: throw ball and hit to partner; B returns ball with high arch close behind net; change after 3 to 5 spikes. 2: throw ball over net (C); direct spike (D); dig attack (E).

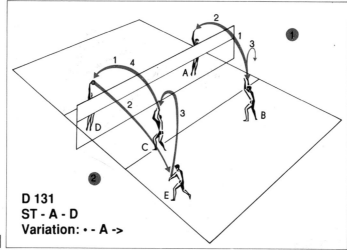

D 131

D 131
ST - A - D
Variation: · - A ->

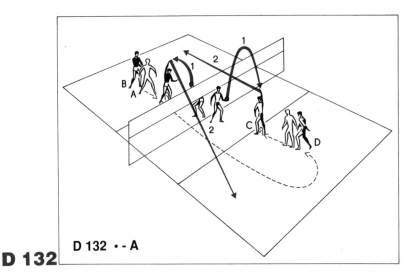

D 132 ·- A

D 132

Attack from backcourt. Throw the ball with a power spike (hit the ball with arm extended when shot becomes more powerful; strive for maximum height for shot and use tactically justifiable risks).

Attack from backcourt. Attack on both sides from different backcourt positions. Jump up high and hit the ball with arm extended. Consider risk of error and hitting power. Attack cross-court from an outside position, as the chance of the ball going out-of-bounds is less.

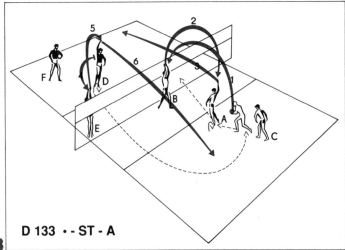

D 133 ·- ST - A

D 133

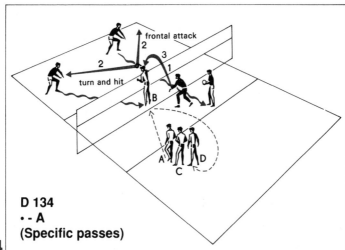

D 134

D 134
• - A
(Specific passes)

Hit "ascending" balls. Coach throws ball short; attacker tries to hit ball in its ascending arch. This drill is best practised with player approaching running up quickly and coach throwing ball underhand up into the hitting arm.

Learning offensive combinations (ascending ball position 3). Developing timing co-ordination between setter and attacker. Practise first with setter at net, then with back-row setter.

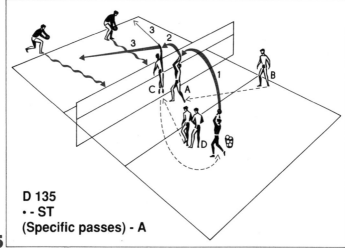

D 135

D 135
• - ST
(Specific passes) - A

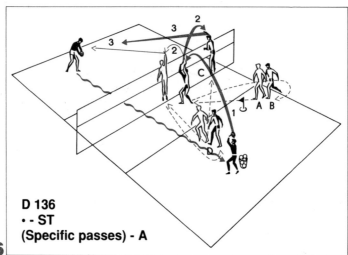

D 136
• - ST
(Specific passes) - A

D 136

Learning offensive combinations. Co-ordination in timing and position between setter and one attacker. Attacker assumes position in front of or behind setter and receives a short set. If ball is passed toward position 3 - attacker behind setter; if pass is toward position 2 - attacker in front of setter.

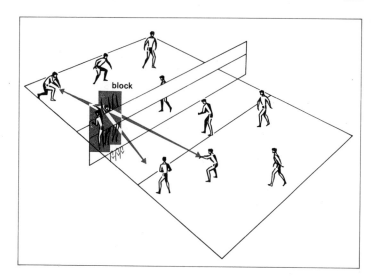

3.5   The Block

3.5.1   General Characteristics

The block can be both *defensive* or *offensive*. It acts as defence against attack by opponents at the net and thus stops the ball falling into the defending court. By reaching over the net players can return the ball directly to the opponents' court or at least lessen force of the ball arriving in their own court. An active offensive block is especially important among experienced players because, in the case of a powerful attack, defence is possible only if the block formation is technically and tactically sound. Effective counter-attacks that score points require good teamwork between block and court defence. The first block defence after a team's own serve is of special importance because it determines whether the team can "neutralize" the opponents' attack, score a point, or gain the initiative for offensive continuation of play.

The effectiveness of the block is determined by the number of players forming the block, their reaching over the net, correct choice and quick movement to the block position, timing of the jump, and players' tactical knowledge and experience. A distinction is made between the various blocking styles in relation to the number of players involved. The main type is the *two-player block*, which, generally speaking, is used for spikes with high passes and when possible against offensive combinations. If a double block formation is not possible, a *one-player block* is formed. Each frontcourt player is responsible for blocking the spike by his or her immediate opponent. In special cases a *three-player block* is formed in the middle of the net (or at outside positions for top league teams). In two- and three-player blocks the player directly across from the attacker forms the block. The player at position 3 is the most active blocker because blocks are made at this position and at both outside positions. For this reason, the best blocker stands at this position or rotates to this position. Functionally, this player is referred to directly as the middle blocker.

Although blocking becomes more relevant to success in the game when hard driven spikes have to be defended, it should be incorporated sooner into the training program. With mini-volleyball ("3 on 3") and "4 on 4", use the one-player block if players are able to attack. If in the game "6 on 6" offensive play is still carried out on a low scale, it is important for tactical training to begin forming a closed two-player block. With this type of block and the others mentioned above, the goal is not an offensive block but rather the formation of a defensive one. It is used to cover a specific area of the court (zone block). Defensive players use the block as a guide for positioning themselves. The positioning of the block and the court defence is dependent on the defensive system chosen.

3.5.2   Teaching the Block

Begin practising the block after all other skills in the game have been practised and especially when hard driven spikes become a part of the play. The one-player block should be followed by the two-player block and team play among all of the frontcourt players. Whereas technical execution is stressed at first (movement towards position of play, block jump without contacting the net and stepping over the line), players learn to co-ordinate a two-player block; they do not form two one-player blocks. After learning the conditions for a zone block (defensive block), players should then quickly learn the different tactical variations for the different types of offensive blocks. Formation of the block is determined largely by opponents' offensive play. For this reason, when learning and perfecting blocking techniques, players must watch opponents continuously (passers, setters attackers) and practise making decisions (determining block position, time of block jump, type of block). Do not practise relatively simple blocking techniques for too long isolated from the game situation.

The number of factors to be considered (assessing offensive possibilities of frontcourt players, following developing offensive patterns, flight path of the set, attacker's arm and hand position, etc.) implies that players must have considerable experience before they can master blocking. Special attention should be devoted to teaching tactical rules.

Tactically correct decisions for blocking may require careful processing of a large amount of information that is sometimes difficult or even impossible to identify. A learning process based only on players' own experiences of trial and error would rarely prove fruitful. With tactical block training athletic demands are also increased.

The learning process should begin with practising the movement sequence without the ball in standing position and moving sideways along the net. This is followed by blocking across the net in conjunction with a stationary and then moving ball.

It is important in all of the drills to co-ordinate movements so that contact with the net is not made. The blocking description that follows now includes the attack. Beginning with the one-player block for spikes with fixed offensive positions and direction for spike, we continue with a two-player block for spikes and finally co-ordinated block play by all of the frontcourt players, whose offensive play becomes more and more variable. Lastly, the training programme branches off into numerous complexities and game forms where blocking is included in the situation-governed movement sequence.

3.5.3   Coaching Tips

The principal problem of block training is the "contradiction" between the need for special training and the strenuous exercising systems which can be boring and rarely result in success. The experience of a successful attack is, for example, a much greater incentive for exercising. Also, the link between execution of movements and its result (assisted by clear instructions for correction) can be established much better when receiving serve or when setting the ball up than when blocking. When receiving serve or setting the ball for attack, players largely determine their actions themselves, being able to process instructions immediately. Successful blocking, however, depends on the number of errors made by opponents and is dictated by chance; the causes of success or failure often cannot clearly be analyzed. Needless to say, all these elements have an influence on the purposeful training process. However, in spite of the difficulties, systematic training must not be neglected.

There is, of course, little sense in having players go through formal block training unenthusiastically, and jumping without putting all of their effort into creating a successful block. Block training always requires self-discipline, persistence and a high level of aggressive play. It is therefore better to change blockers after few but adequate plays or after a suitable relaxation period and have them begin another short series of block jumps. Combining blocking with actions leading up to and following the block makes practice more interesting and reduces the monotony of successive blocking.

In order to meet the physical demands of the game, longer series of drills for blocking should be implemented periodically. In offensive training, one should always consider how to include practising blocking at the same time. Players, however, should not change directly between offence and block. A continuous series of jumping movements is to be avoided by inserting a "rest period" into the drill (e.g., players do setting, passing, retrieving balls). Since it is by no means customary in training practice, it is perhaps worth remembering that coaches should observe and correct blocking from behind the court if possible.

3.5.4   Tactical Rules

- In ready position close to net (hands roughly at shoulder height in front of body) watch for the opponent's offensive play as it develops (defence on court, setting attacker's play), try to anticipate the offensive position, an decide if a block formation is at all necessary.
- Watch the trajectory of the ball carefully and gauge the possibilities for the offensive players and move quickly to probable blocking position.
- In principle, block all hard driven spikes (up to 2.5 m from net). Full participation in blocking is a feature of tactical discipline.
- Try to maintain a two-player block if pass is high enough and if blocking position has been identified in time. Player already in blocking position forms the block (blocks ball); the approaching players "close" the block (eliminating probable line of attack).
- Choose take-off spot so that main hitting direction can be covered when blocking. At outside positions (2 and 4) only block balls outside the court and directly if close to the net; with normal balls it is better to block too far inside than too far outside.
- For spikes up to one metre away from the net, form an offensive block (arms over the net, toward the ball); otherwise form a zone block.
- With a single-player block bring both hands as close as possible to the ball. With a two-player block at position 3, "inner" hands are on ball, "outer" hands are closed facing inwards (curved).
- The higher the ball is set and the farther it is away from the net, the more delay in the block jump (maximum height at point of contact of the ball in the spiker's hand).
- When blocking against an offensive take off with attacker or even somewhat sooner, bend legs and arms in order to reach the ball quickly. Speed is more important than blocking height.
- Go for effective block formation. Try to achieve "attack impact" (reach

over net, push, cupping hands around ball); or use zone block to provide a basis for defence. A decision to forego blocking for backcourt defence is tactically justifiable if it is indicated clearly and in good time.

● Try to prevent attacker from "wiping off" by turning outer hands inwards or bringing hand around from the side. Pull hands away when attacker's intentions are clear.

● Do not reach over the net before attacker contacts the ball; in so doing you only lose maximum possible blocking height.

● Spread and tense fingers when blocking and place forearms close to net so that ball cannot be hit into the block. Bring arms quickly down after block contact.

● Use arms actively over the net (sideways as well). In the case of tactical (softer) shots cover all possible lines of attack by spreading out the block and moving sideways. For hard driven spikes place hands closer together to keep block tightly closed.

● Be ready for play immediately after blocking. Turn and watch court while landing. If you do not block proceed immediately to your defence or block coverage.

● Determine precisely who is to form a two-player block at position 3 (mostly players at positions 3 and 4). Also make sure that excellent attackers face outstanding blockers, or reorganize the block by switching players accordingly.

3.5.5   Drill Pool

Preparatory drills: D 137 to D 147.
One- and two-player blocks against spikes: D 148 to D 156.

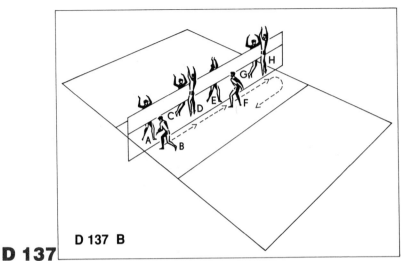

D 137 B

D 137

Touching palms of partner's hands above net. Press hands close together above net without contacting it. Variation: while jumping follow horizontal changes in position of partner's hands or block simulated spikes.

Passing balls over net to player. Pairs of players pass balls to each other after standing jump or after a lateral step. Pass ball directly into hands.

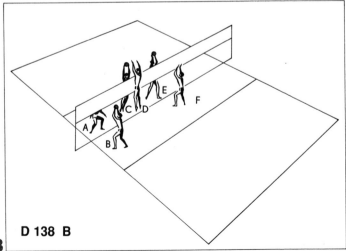

D 138 B

D 138

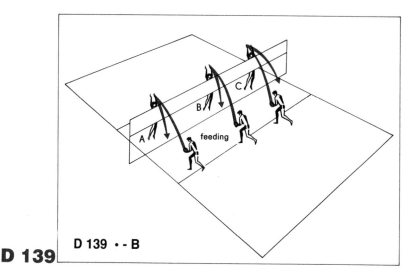

D 139 D 139 · - B

Block balls thrown by player. Block balls thrown flat over edge of net. Reach over and push downward with fingers spread, then bring arms back quickly. Variation: combine block with defence of the blocked ball. Change after blocking 3 to 5 times.

Prepare for single-player block. Use a stationary ball or a ball moved to the right and left. Throw ball between two players above the edge of the net; the two players attempt to block the ball toward their opponents' court.

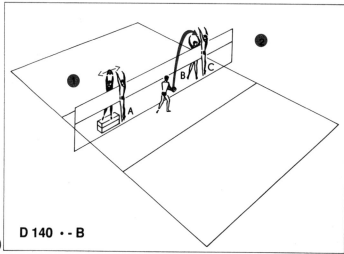

D 140 D 140 · - B

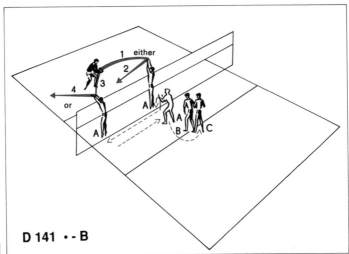

D 141

D 141 • - B

Single-player blocks in rapid succession. Coach throws to various points over the net; player A runs quickly to block position, takes a break step, turns and faces net while jumping and blocks. Jump vertically; do not move horizontally.

One- and two-player blocks with stationary and flying ball. 1: Run to block position and block stationary ball. Outside player takes the ball, inside player "closes" the block. Spread fingers and cup hands around the ball. 2: Player C tosses ball for blocker D to direct into centre of court.

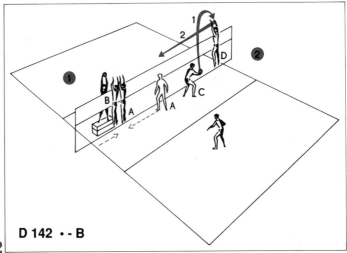

D 142

D 142 • - B

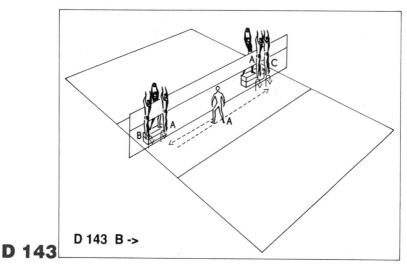

D 143 B ->

D 143

Close two-player block quickly. Player A jumps together with B or C. Block jointly; do not form two single-player blocks. Do not turn towards the net until last two steps; during jump do not move outwards.

Prepare for two-player block. 1: Player B blocks stationary ball. If ball goes to outside, player places left hand around the ball (curved). 2: Both pairs of blockers try to push the ball into opponents' court.

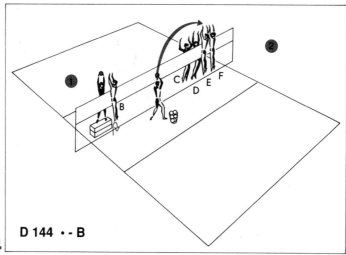

D 144 · - B

D 144

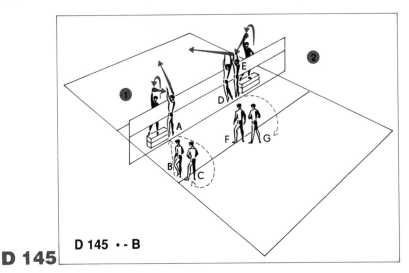

D 145

D 145 • - B

Block spike by coach who stands on box. Learning one- and two-player block against spikes under simplified conditions. Determine angle of spike first, then block different spike techniques or directions.

Block lob by partner. Player throws ball to self, close to net and hits offspeed spike; opponent blocks. Blocker watches attacker carefully; delays jump. Head remains behind arms and do not close eyes.

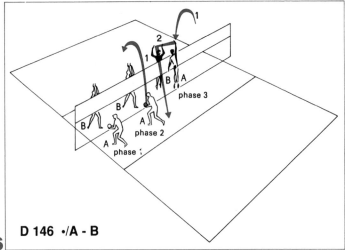

D 146

D 146 •/A - B

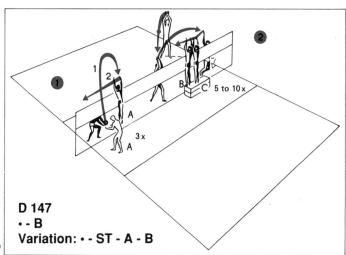

D 147
• - B
Variation: • - ST - A - B

D 147

Single-player blocks in rapid succession and two-player block on box. 1: Place three balls in a row. Jump to maximum height. 2: Practise blocking without jumping. Outside player should be turned towards net.

One-player block with fixed spike angle. Spike with medium high passes. Block knows spike angle and blocks ball. Delay jump of block (after attacker's take-off). After blocking 3 to 5 times, change. Do not set balls too far from net.

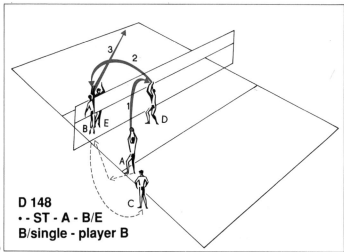

D 148
• - ST - A - B/E
B/single - player B

D 148

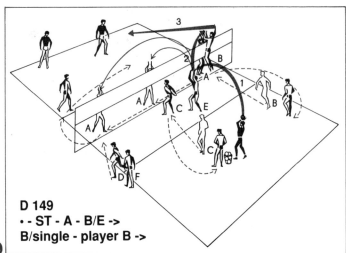

D 149
• - ST - A - B/E ->
B/single - player B ->

D 149

Blocking successive spikes from three positions. Players B, C and D-attack; A blocks three times. Begin when setter contacts the ball. Practise at pace so that effective blocks are possible.

Anticipate spike angle and block. Spike with medium to high passes and with body turned; anticipate spike direction and position block accordingly.

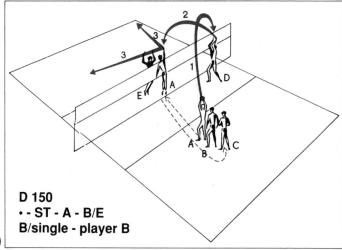

D 150
• - ST - A - B/E
B/single - player B

D 150

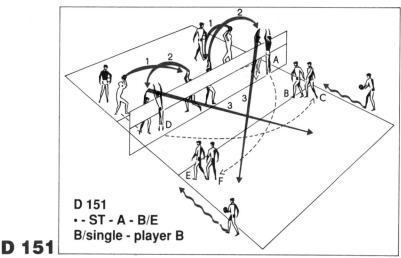

D 151
• - ST - A - B/E
B/single - player B

D 151

Block spikes. Spikes from positions 2 and 4 with pre-determined offensive direction. Block alternates between both positions. Practise continuously with numerous repetitions in order to consolidate movements.

Two-player block for spikes from outside positions. Spikes with high passes from position 4; formation of two-player block at position 2. Players F and D move to position 3 to form block; begin movement when ball is set.

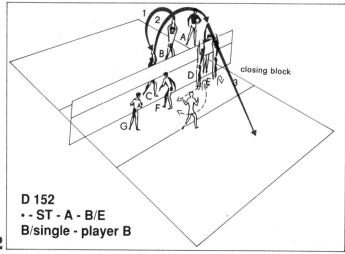

closing block

D 152
• - ST - A - B/E
B/single - player B

D 152

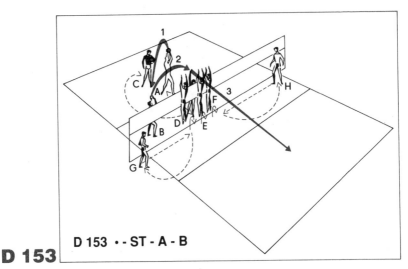

D 153

D 153 · - ST - A - B

Block spikes in threes at position 3. Spike with high passes. Centre blocker E practises several times at the appropriate position. Two players each take turns running alternately from outside positions inward and "close" the three-player block.

Block stationary ball and cover. Player on top of box holds ball over the net and drops it into opponents' court after block contact. Blockers recover the ball. A, B and C supply balls.

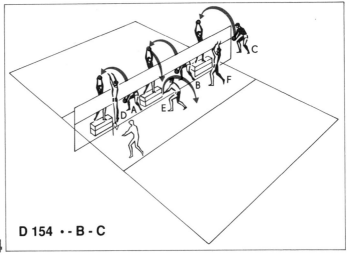

D 154

D 154 · - B - C

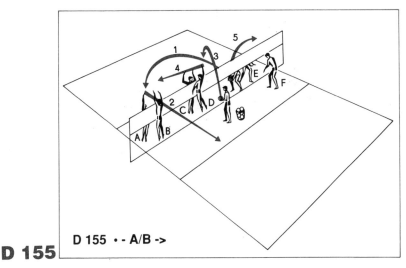

D 155 · - A/B ->

D 155

Spike or block. Two rows of blockers stand across from each other. Depending upon how ball is thrown, the players spike or block with reduced preparation time. Co-ordinate your actions when throwing balls.

Ready to recover immediately after block. After one-player block return to position as free frontcourt player. Ready position, then practise so that after block short diagonal spikes can be recovered.

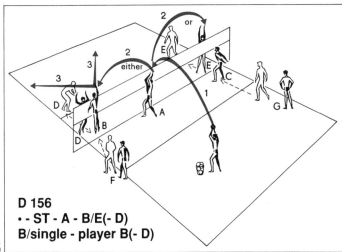

D 156
· - ST - A - B/E(- D)
B/single - player B(- D)

D 156

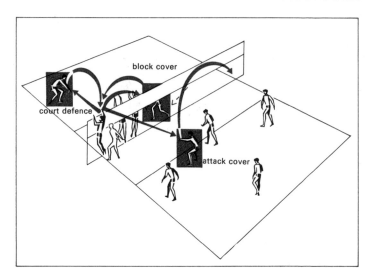

3.6   The Court Defence

3.6.1   General Characteristics

Together with blocking, court defence is one of the most important means for defending against spikes by opponents. Successful court defence prevents not only loss of points and service, but it is above all the first stage in the formation of your team's offensive. Court defence is contingent upon the actions by opposing attackers, and the formation of the backcourt players around the block. A good defence also allows the players to prepare their own counter-attack to the best advantage. The numerous possibilities for the attack and the time needed to execute the play—often reduced to split seconds—place great demands on concentration and speed of reaction. Players must concentrate completely and be constantly thinking about their play so that their actions complement collective defensive play.

Success is determined by how well a player learns to anticipate. In conjunction with tactical discipline, defensive success is increased by the ability to anticipate early of the position, variation, and direction of the attack. Although it is possible in many cases to anticipate the correct defensive position, this is not possible in all cases. Each player, however, is always responsible for trying to save all difficult balls with swift reflex movement and maximum aggressive play.

Despite collective decisions for court defence, individual defensive play in the game is also critical, its technical execution as different as the variety of tactical demands. The most effective method is the *two-handed underhand dig (bump)* in both standing and falling (rolling) positions. With correct positional play bumping must be as frequent a part as possible in all defensive plays, since recovery to the setter is crucial to a systematic offensive formation. Ideally, the ball is bumped with the player's body behind the ball. Even hard driven spikes can be recovered relatively accurately. Frequently, however, the balls are hit off to the player's side, making it necessary to know the two-handed sidearm recovery. When digging balls flying away from a player, the players must attempt to save the ball by running quickly and digging or passing the ball as they are diving or falling (often having to use one hand). As distance travelled increases, recovery becomes more uncertain and inaccurate.

In addition to actual court defence (direct defensive plays and saving the ball after opponents' attack), we must consider two other types of court defence as part of the entire complex of court defence training - *attack* and *block coverage*. Spikes often get blocked back into the players' own half of the court and can rarely be played by the attacker himself. The attacker is then covered by several teammates. In principle, all players take part in covering. They organize short-distance coverage (2 to 3 players) and long-distance coverage (1 to 2 players). Different coverage variations are possible, depending upon the intensity of the game and tactics used, although specific rules cannot be determined for each particular case.

For reasons similar to attack coverage, we shall refer to block coverage as a specific type of court defence. Offspeed hits, tips or deflected shots near the block are often difficult for blockers to recover themselves. Therefore, decisions are made in the tactical system regarding block coverage (e.g., system with the player in position 6 pulled up on court; coverage by backcourt players at positions 5 and 1; special instructions for single-, three-, and two-player blocks at position 3).

Following the rules of court defence, players act and resolve the situation appropriately in both types, often using methods similar to volleying or bumping. *Saving net balls* is a type of recovery that also plays a role in defensive training.

3.6.2   Teaching the Court Defence

Beginners unskilled in spiking should defend the ball with overhead passes. As they improve their attack play and learn how to spike, players proceed to bump for defence. Since balls are being played to them at a fairly low speed, they should attempt to defend by body movement without moving their feet. Before graduating to drills in near-competiton conditions, players are taught, either by exercising with partners or under the guidance of the coach, to defend the ball and to move to their respective play position. Team play with the next player is gradually incorporated into the drills, along with defensive plays requiring players to change directions (see drills for court defence).

Digging hard driven spikes also requires intensive preparation because their recovery differs greatly from service reception and from underarm court passes. Coaches also play a decisive role in the learning process here because they can control the hitting strength perfectly and are more apt to hit directly to the player. Practising against a wall, as described in the section on service reception (D 13-D 34), serves as good preparation. Players should not, however, spend too much time practising hitting balls directly to players. Instead, they should learn lateral defence with balls delivered by the coach, who varies his throws and strikes. The coach should also insist on the players moving to the ball and taking up correct play positions.

Special methodical steps must be taken for learning *defensive styles in falling (sprawling) position*. Floor drills using soft mats, with and without balls tend to make players' less worried about landing and prevent injuries from occurring. As soon as players have mastered landing techniques, they begin to recover balls thrown flat by coach or partner in a falling position. Care must be taken in all the drills that the ball is played to the player so that it is readily reachable; perfect motor execution is then possible. Players must also remember to practise from the beginning how to recover from both sides of the body.

The chief means used in perfecting court defence is the so-called "Japanese" defensive training and the related variations. These techniques stress the use of different defensive styles. Coaches can simulate tactical demands in accordance with competition (team play with neighbouring players, change from positional defence, rotation to the next position, block coverage). By varying training methods the coach promotes fluid footwork. These types of court defence drills form an integral component of training and should be used with experienced players.

After having learned court defence under simplified conditions a great deal of time is devoted to digging spikes (coach stands on box feeding balls; teammates spike normally). We shall begin with position-specific defence in the prime hitting direction, then vary direction for hitting and widen the defensive player's sphere of action (block coverage, relation to next position). We move from defence by individual players to drills that involve team play in groups and finally among the entire team. Blocking is gradually incorporated into the drills in order to simulate almost exactly future competitive conditions in simple drill drills.

Defensive play is characterized, in particular, by the rapid switch from the previous action to court defence and the transition to the next play. Recovering, setting and covering, moving away from the net and defence digging (frontcourt players not part of block), digging and attacking are typical combinations of plays that can be trained in different drills.

The drills in which court defence is practised separately or in conjunction with blocking as well as the last group of drills mentioned gradually come to include setting and spiking. The emphasis is placed on target-related defensive plays as the basis for optimum offensive preparation.

In *attack* and *block coverage* as well a few drills are included at first for learning the typical features of the movements. For learning correct positional play and movement coaches normally have players complete drills that simulate these specific types. It is recommended in all cases that coverage tasks (attack or block) be made an integral part of court defence training, even if players have not yet mastered spiking. The last step in training is actual defence on the court within specified collective tactics under competitive conditions.

More advanced players should use drills where they need to recover hard-hit balls. While a number of "specific forms" of court defence (for example, recovery of net balls)should be exercised in a purpose-related manner, these drills should not become the focal point of the training session.

3.6.3   Coaching Tips

Court defence makes heavy demands on the physical fitness, mental tactics, and technical coordination of players and on their will power and morale. The complexity of these demands makes court defence a difficult component to learn in the game and players can master it only through long-term training. This is why laying the proper foundations for training court defence (movement towards the ball, position in relation to the ball, conduct in the tactical system), together with learning passing (passing on court, setting) and passing serves is so important.

The sequence of movements demand of players to exercise separately the different variants of defence and with a great number of repetitions. Individual components in the plays should have been perfected before greater demands are made. Coaches should avoid combining motor skill development with maximum aggressive play at the very beginning of training. The same applies to the attempt to develop motor speed when players cannot perform the defensive plays that follow.

Coaching skills therefore play an important role particularly in court defence training. The coach should be able to throw the ball or hit it to the player, who, pushed to the limit, must execute the play but must maintain the same level of quality. The danger exists that, when practising a specific skill isolated from its other components, players practise abstractly, and thus in a manner unsuitable for actual court defence in its various game situations. However, when coaches guide the practice session by spiking from top of boxes, and when they concentrate on position-specific aspects when teaching court defence, the way is already paved for more complex training. When arranging the drills coaches must ensure that players complete only a few successive repetitions or that several players alternate practising continuously. Players must meet requirements in speed, reaction, and concentration without affecting their performance; otherwise, players will learn plays unsuitable for competition.

Once players practise court defence in conjunction with opponents' attack and blocking, the number of direct ball passes often noticeably diminishes (error of attack, error or success of block, etc.). This complicates and prolongs the training process. On the other hand, it shows that it is not only direct ball defence that will be effective through training; training has to include the team-work of other players, even though they may not be involved in direct ball play. It is the duty of the coach again and again to challenge players to control and correct their play. He will succeed as their tactical knowledge improves.

It is important in court defensive training to work with as many balls as possible and to ensure a fluid drill progression that is well-organized. To ensure a steady supply of balls, players not directly involved in practising must help out and spur on active defensive players. The coach may organize various complex exercises and play forms for longer play by feeding a new ball himself each time the play is interrupted.

3.6.4   Tactical Rules

- Try to anticipate early in the play from which net position opponents will attack and which offensive variation you can expect. Judge the most likely type and direction of attack, and determine from the front line players' positions (block position or block screen) where you can defend the ball best. You can increase chances of success if you move to your defending position quickly.
- Decide, depending upon the type, direction and speed of the spike which type of court defence will be the most effective. Pursue easy and high balls, and recover them in standing position or even using the

overhead pass as often as possible. Recover hard driven spikes crouched, with both arms extended. Recover in a diving or rolling position only when it is not possible to do so standing, and always attempt to play the balls using both arms.

• Always be prepared for a fake from the block.At all times be a lert and ready to change the defence you intended to play.

• Recover the ball high to the setter, not too close to the net and especially not to the opponent. Playing safe is more important than accuracy with difficult balls. In these cases recover the ball high and to the centre court.

• Ensure that balls far from the net are not hit hard into the centre court area. When a block covers the attacker, power driven spikes are highly unlikely. In these situations, position yourself in the centre and be prepared to move quickly.

• Never run forwards too soon or automatically. If an opposing attacker plays ball over you, your chances of effective defence are slim.

• Try to see your neighbouring players using your peripheral vision and co-ordinate your actions with theirs. Compensate for any errors by teammates with aggressive play. Hurry and help to cover for your partner when balls are being saved outside of the court.

• If defensive responsibility is not clear, the player who can react the quickest must carry through with the action.

• Never assume a ball is lost. Be persistent and try to play even balls that seem out of reach.

• Be prepared for the next play immediately after each defensive play.

3.6.5   Drill Pool

Preparatory drills: D 157 to D 160.
Defence on court under simplified conditions (movement towards ball, technical execution) drills: D 161 to D 168.
Drills for different types of defence: D 169 to D 172.
Position-specific defence drills: D 173 to D 183.
Court defence with coach/group drills: D 184 to D 190.
Attack coverage/block coverage drills: D 191 to D 202.
Drills for specific defensive situations: D 203 to D 207.

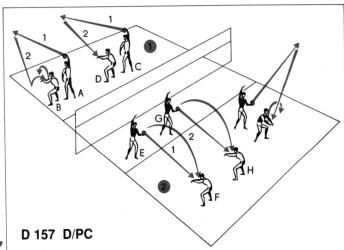

D 157   **D 157 D/PC**

Learning two-handed dig in standing position. Dig rebound from wall; bump balls back hit by partner. Hit the ball flat and hard so that ball must be played in crouched defensive position.

Non-stop spiking - digging. Attack from standing position; dig, overhead pass, attack by second player, etc. Count each defensive play out loud. Who can do the most repetitions? Variation: A hits, B recovers.

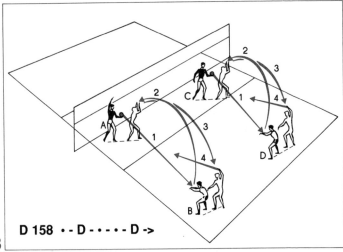

D 158   **D 158 • - D - • • • • D ->**

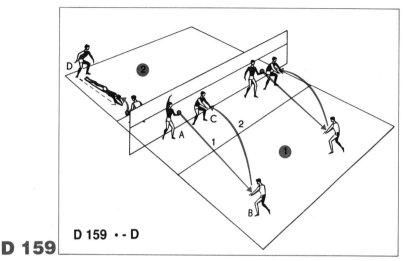

D 159

D 159 · - D

Defensive recovery with chanding direction of pass and with forward dive. Bump spike by player A directly to C. Stand with body behind ball and bump ball forward. Run towards the ball first, then recover it with forward dive.

Practise recovery in pairs. Hit ball to partner, bump up into the air and spike it back or bump to a third player. If played to third player (B), B sets to A who hits it back. Count out loud each time bump is made.

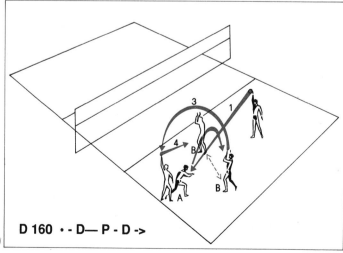

D 160

D 160 · - D— P - D ->

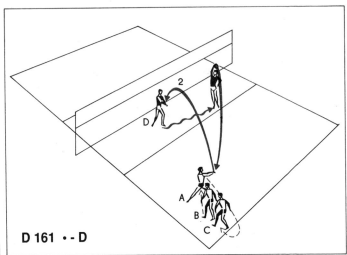

D 161

D 161 • - D

Cross-court dig of spike. Ball is played to position 2; two-handed bump in standing or sprawling position. Emphasis on correct execution of movement. Avoid situations where player only stands in one spot; emphasize proper movement.

Side recovery in standing position. Coach (in position 3) hits the ball to side of defensive player. Bump with change of direction as well (toward position 2). When playing ball tilt closed arms off to one side at ball contact. Move arms in opposite direction to ball flight and give.

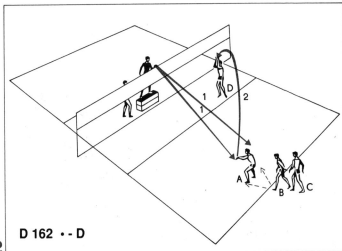

D 162

D 162 • - D

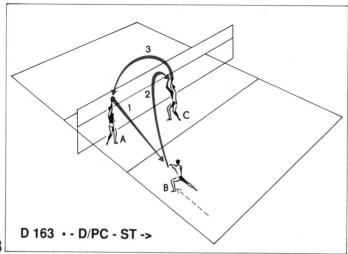

D 163

D 163 · - D/PC - ST ->

Recover to frontcourt passer. Controlled shots to position 5 - make two-handed bump to position 3 - passes to position 4. Develop spiking and defensive differentiation ability by varying force of shot. Also feed ball variably. Variation: 2 to 3 players take turns recovering.

Continuous digging. Practise in groups of three; A spikes down the sideline; B bumps ball to C, sets A and repeats attack. How many plays can you complete withoutut interruption?

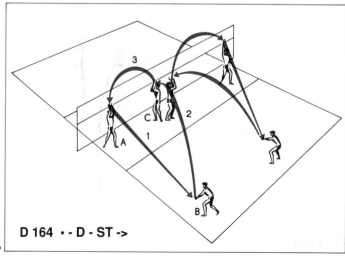

D 164

D 164 · - D - ST ->

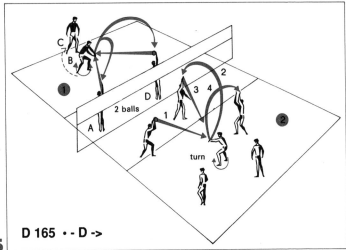

D 165

D 165 · - D ->

Digging and change direction of ball. Player B takes turns bumping to players A and D. Always bump to outside frontcourt player. Ensure good footwork on the spot (be ready in position on balls of feet).

Take over next position and recover diagonal spikes. Defensive player begins in position 6 moves to the right and then left and bumps to position 3. Try to pass placed spikes with body movement while remaining stationary.

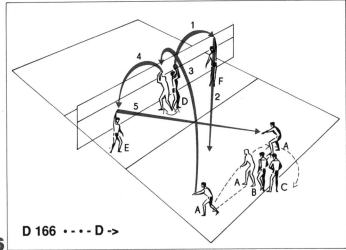

D 166

D 166 · - · - D ->

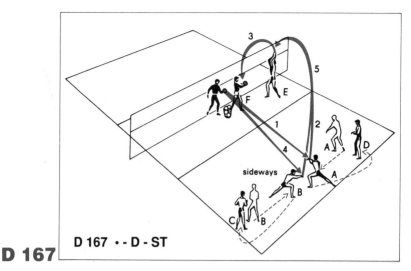

D 167

D 167 · - D - ST

Take over next position and dig a rapid series of shots. In rapid succession coach hits to position 6; alternate between taking over positions 1 and 5 and bumping to position 2. Use two-handed bumping techniques as much as possible. Variation: after each play rotate to the next position.

React quickly and recover. On the signal, player A turns around and bumps ball to the right or left; pass is hidden by box.

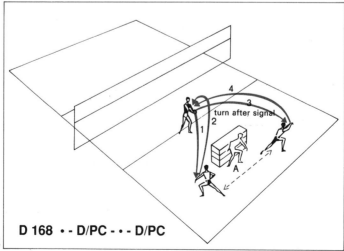

D 168

D 168 · - D/PC - · · - D/PC

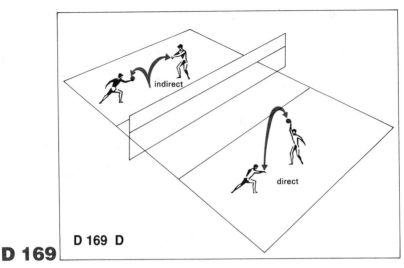

D 169

D 169 D

Develop "feeling" for the ball for defensive plays. One- or two-handed lateral bump using one arm or both arms, with direct or indirect floor contact. Pay special attention to keeping arms stretched and rigid.

Digging to the right and left falling or rolling sideways. Run to right or left; bump while falling sideways (roll over as well). Simplify drill by placing mats on the court. Exercise in fluid succession: approach ball - lunge - play ball - roll over.

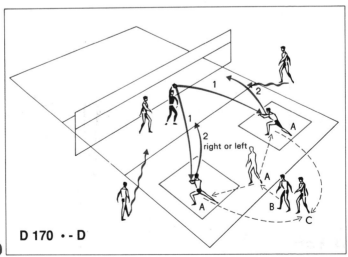

D 170

D 170 · - D

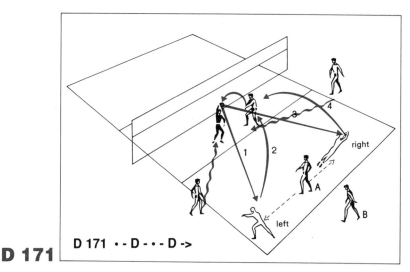

D 171

D 171 · - D - · - D ->

Take over next position and save balls. Two-handed bump in falling position. Coach feeds the ball such that it can still be reached with maximum effort. Combine play with speed requirements.

Recover ball with forward dive. 1: Bounce ball several times and prevent next contact of ball with court. 2: Coach feeds low balls sideways which the player defends to the passer as he dives forwards.

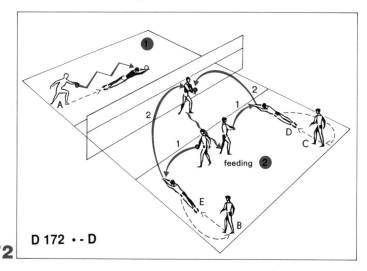

D 172 · - D

D 172

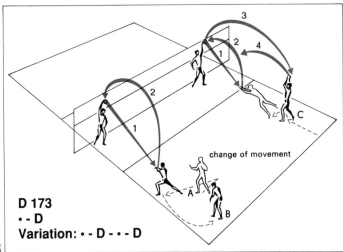

D 173

Dig ball directly to frontcourt player. Court defence developing individual motor skills. Dig easy shots while moving towards the ball; generate accurate passes towards the net.

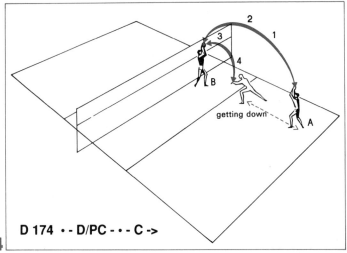

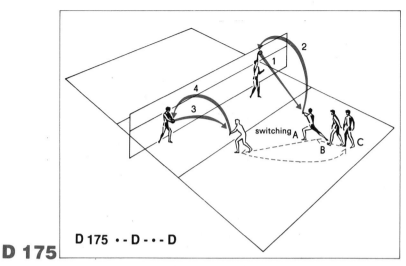

D 175 ·-D-·-D

D 175

Digging twice in a row. Bump controlled power spikes directly back to hitter, then run towards centre of court and save a difficult ball. Try to save with two-handed bump when digging difficult balls (in falling position).

Digging three times in a row. After each play be ready immediately for the next action. Decide on the next play and assume new playing position with quick, flat steps.

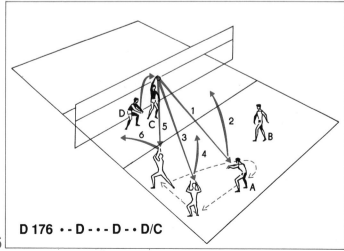

D 176 ·-D-·-D-·-D/C

D 176

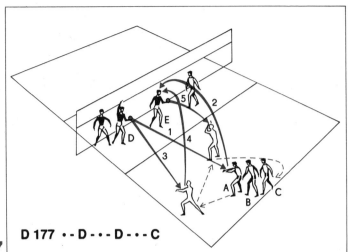

D 177

D 177 · - D - · - D - · · - C

Dig twice, pass once sequence. Player A bumps at position 6, moves to position 5 and also bumps line attack to position 3, then overhead pass across short distance back to position 3. Ensure fluid, efficient leg activity. **Dig two balls in a row**. Starting in position 6, move to position 5. 1: Run for the ball and make two-handed bump standing (falling) toward position 4 (player D). 2: Save the difficult ball tossed or hit from player E. Change net and defensive positions (i.e., starting at position 1 and moving to position 6).

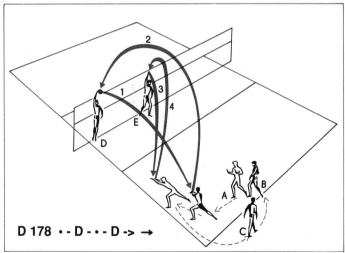

D 178

D 178 · - D - · - D -> →

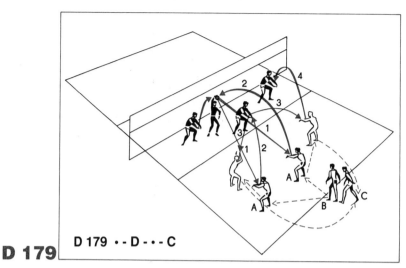

D 179 D 179 ·-D-··-C

Defensive digging - pass after variable balls. From position 6 cover larger area of the court. Pay close attention to fluid footwork when moving to different playing positions.

Control defensive area. Dig spikes coming cross-court from opponents' power position. Do not lunge forward; always return to starting position in backcourt. After each dig be ready to resume play immediately.

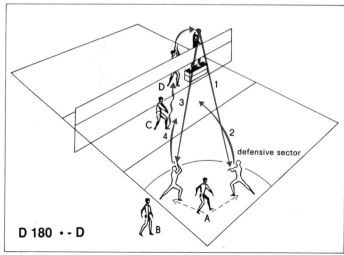

D 180 D 180 ·-D

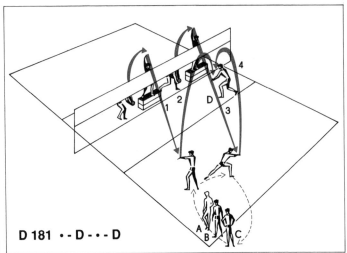

D 181

D 181 · · D · · · D

Dig twice in a row. Concentrate on accurate defence to the ball passing position. Improve court defence at specific positions; direct attack to neighbouring position (combining position - defence - penetration).

Dig and pass in succession. Dig power spike; pass soft ball from opponent - accurate pass. Differentiate between "giving" when defending and "sensitive" ball handling as you play court passes.

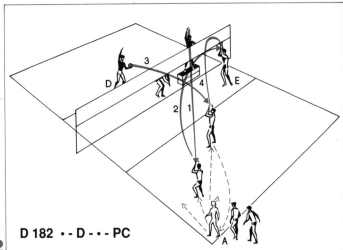

D 182

D 182 · · D · · · PC

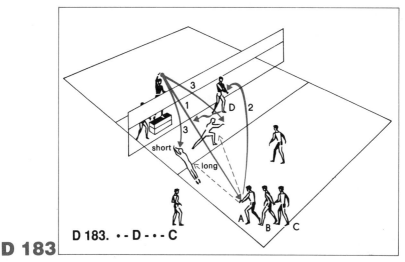

D 183. ·-D-···C

D 183

Return ball accurately. Coach varies shots hit or thrown from box (position defence or taking over at positions 4 and 3); players A, B and C take turns bumping directly to player F (positions 3, 2).

Return ball accurately to coach. Divide players into two groups of three, with two players working together. Coach hits at D who bumps to A, who passes to coach; Coach hits to B who bumps to E etc. Perform the drill continuously. When mistake is made, throw in a new ball.

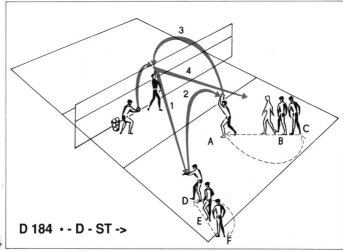

D 184 ·-D-ST->

D 184

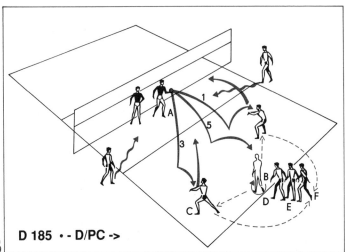

D 185

D 185 · - D/PC ->

Returning ball to coach after rebound. Coach throws balls indirectly and irregularly to backcourt. From position 6 approach quickly and bump the ball accurately back to coach. Move into playing position quickly.

Digging line and cross-court attacks non-stop. Players E and B hit ball irregularly in down the line or in cross-court direction; two-handed bump to A, who sets immediately. Variation: defensive players change position after each play.

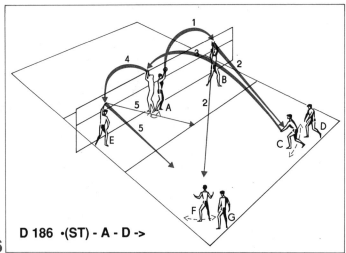

D 186

D 186 ·(ST) - A - D ->

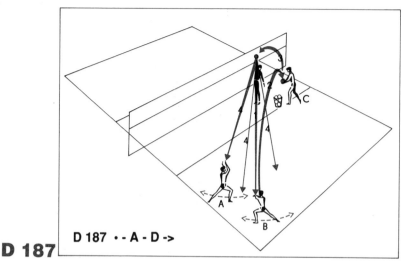

D 187

D 187 · - A - D ->

Bump in co-ordination with next player. Coach hits balls cross-court; co-ordinated defensive plays between players A and B at the crucial link between defence by the frontcourt player and defensive player at position 5.

Digging in threes. Coach hits ball to one player of a group of three. Coach varies the spikes and surprise players with changes in direction. Defensive players must concentrate and be ready for any type of hit.

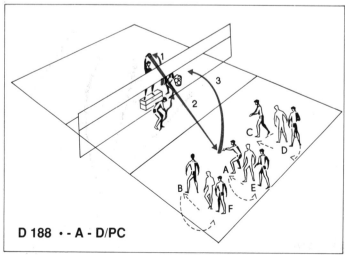

D 188

D 188 · - A - D/PC

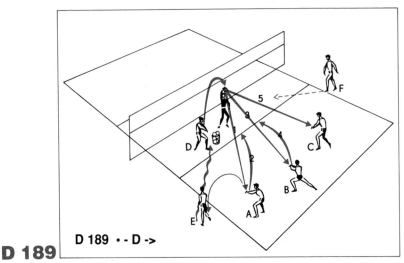

D 189 · - D ->

D 189

Non-stop defensive action in threes. Coach hits to key points in defensive area; players move fast to the back court where they form the defence line. After court defence to the coach, players move back quickly to their respective positions.

Developing concentration and quickly changing to next dig. Bump in threes; frontcourt players vary spikes, taking turns hitting three balls irregularly to defensive players. Use peripheral vision when digging and try to anticipate where next spike will come from.

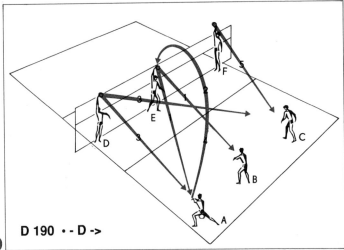

D 190 · - D ->

D 190

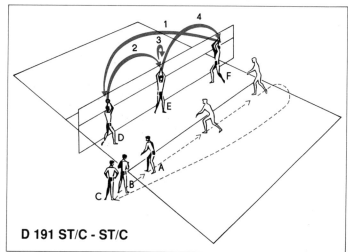

D 191   **D 191 ST/C - ST/C**

Remain at height of ball. Players D, E, and F play ball to each other at the net; A, B and C follow the ball. Assume ready position for block coverage wherever a frontcourt player passes to himself. Variation: play ball to covering player (lob overhead pass).

Approach and cover. Preparatory drill for attack coverage. A either plays ball immediately to C or simulates a blocked ball (he plays ball in a straight line at an oblique angle downwards). Player covering crouches during approach.

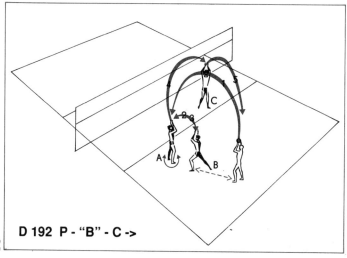

D 192   **D 192 P - "B" - C ->**

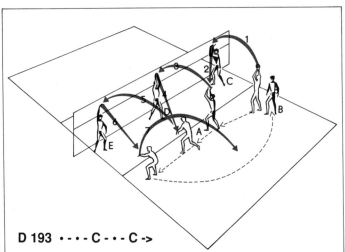

D 193

D 193 · - · - C - · - C ->

Block coverage three times in a row. Frontcourt players simulate blocked balls or tips into frontcourt area by offspeeds or variable overhead passes. A bumps twice to next frontcourt position and bumps third ball up high to centre court.

Teaching coverage play. Backcourt players D, E, and F move quickly back and forth when the ball is played to their frontcourt players. When running forward they crouch down. Variation: periodic passes to the player who is covering.

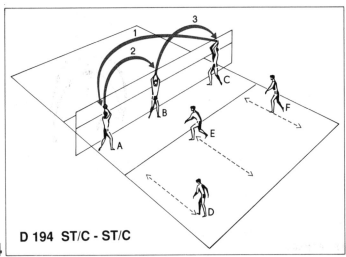

D 194

D 194 ST/C - ST/C

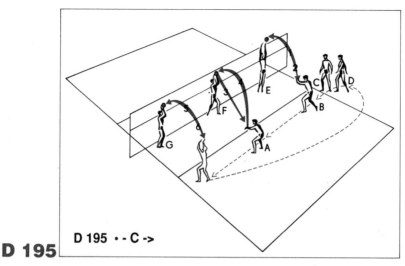

D 195 · - C ->

D 195

Recover three times in a row. A, B, and C move sideways across the court and save difficult balls. Move sideways, remain low, recover quickly, etc. Play ball up into the air so that a set for attack is possible.

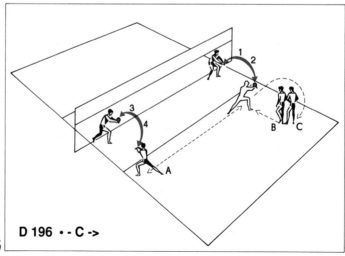

D 196 · - C ->

D 196

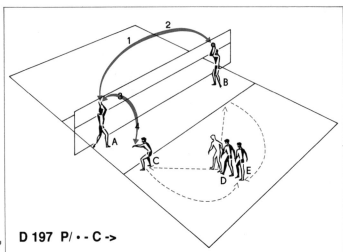

D 197

D 197 P/ • - C ->

Coverage with "6-man up". Players A and B pass the ball to each other at the net and, on signal or without warning, simulate a blocked rebound. Players who are covering (C, D, and E) react attentively and play directly back to players A or B.

React quickly during block coverage. Restriction of player's view by concealing different passes (drape cover over net); react quickly and bump to player D. Prepare for block coverage as "6-man up".

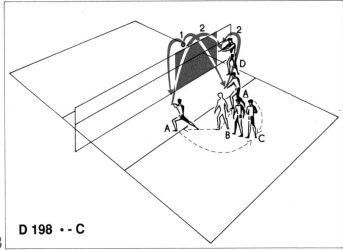

D 198

D 198 • - C

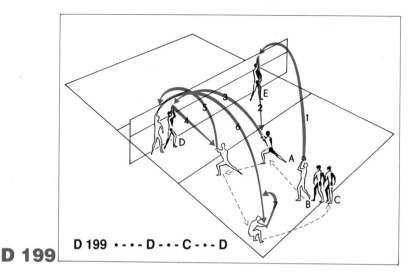

D 199

D 199 · - · · D - · · C - · · D

Recover three times in rapid succession. Improve different defensive skills in conjunction with tasks set to the player to increase his speed. Run quickly to play position first, then bump.

Digging a variety of spikes by coach. First dig accurately from your position, next defend at positions 4 and 3 (prepare to recover ball while block is covered by back players).

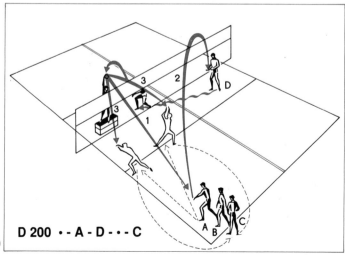

D 200

D 200 · - · A - D - · · · C

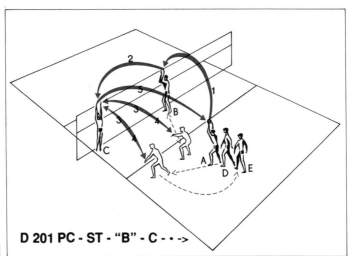

D 201

D 201 PC - ST - "B" - C - • ->

Two-player cover. Recovery of various blocked balls in frontcourt with the aid of player at position 3. Communicate to avoid misunderstanding.

Combine defence and setting, then cover attack in pairs. Players A and B hit to position 5; C, D, and E bump to position 3. A sets to position 4. F plays ball back flat or lets it drop from hands. Passers and defensive players cover.

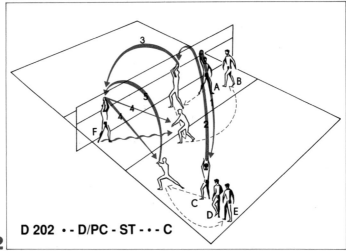

D 202

D 202 • - D/PC - ST - • • - C

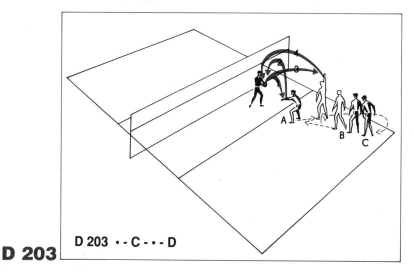

D 203

D 203 • - C - • - D

Recovering high block rebounds. Coach throws first ball short; player A runs forward and bumps, then immediately receives another ball played back overhead, which can only be recovered by jumping up and using one hand. Play with fist or heel of the hand.

Digging "overplayed" balls. At the moment the ball is thrown player makes a quick turn and "moves towards the ball". Coach combines court defence with demands made upon the speed of the players and his co-ordination skills.

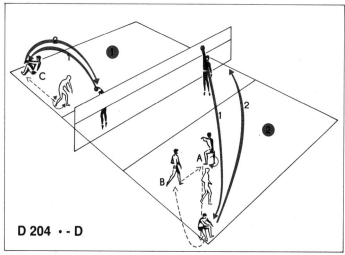

D 204

D 204 • - D

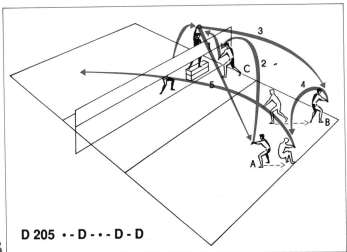

D 205

D 205 · - D - · - D - D

Help teammate when saving difficult balls. Coach spikes the first ball to either A or B, who pass or dig to player C; player C direct bumps to coach who makes second ball a difficult one. B saves the ball. A helps him and bumps the ball over the net.

"Recovering" net balls. Player A throws the ball into the net; B bumps it immediately into opponents' half or plays it to A such that A can at least still make an effective offensive pass.

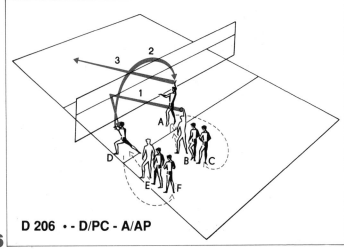

D 206

D 206 · - D/PC - A/AP

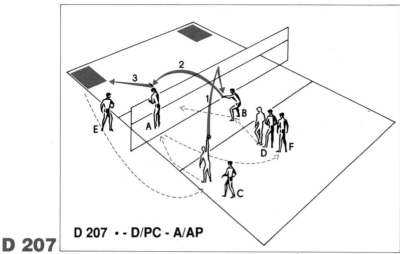

D 207 | D 207 · - D/PC - A/AP

Playing net balls. A drives the ball into the net; B tries to play rebound high enough up into the air so that A can still spike the ball. Do not act hastily when playing the ball from the net. Spike carefully; with difficult balls use controlled offensive play.

4 Integrated Drills

Integrated drills combine several technical or tactical elements of a game situation or phase. They form the *core of near-competition training*. In order to ensure that they are taught efficiently as a unit, techniques and tactics are incorporated into training after players have learned the main forms of individual game elements. Precise systematization is very difficult because practising with emphasis on a particular element in near-competition form is possible only in conjunction with other elements.

In *individual integrated drills* a player completes several technical and tactical tasks in game-like sequence. Drills in which groups of players in game-like situations on one half of the court complete a series of repetitions involving different technical executions that are also complex in nature (such as playing the ball - passing - setting: "Japanese" court defence).

In *game phase drills* emphasis is placed on completing game-related series of actions, taking into consideration individual and collective tactical behaviour and collective effort to ensure that the attack is completed successfully. Several game phases are also combined by "natural" or organized transitions. As a preliminary to these drills, intermediate steps can be taken by detaching parts of the game phases from exercising and producing a simpler sequence, such as, block - court defence - setting.

In *game flowing drills,* movement of ball and players is predetermined. It is important for players to do as many repetitions as possible to become proficient in technique. The flow of play is maintained by the players applying sub-maximal power (attack) and by the coach feeding balls to them as errors occur.

In *non-stop drilling* (rapid action sequences) athletes work primarily at improving specific athletic skills (speed/agility) when using plays familiar to them. The interval training principle should be followed here.

Complex drills can be used in many different ways. Initially it is advisable to get the players to visualise the flow of exercising by practising throwing and catching the ball. to develop game-related skills, players practise feasible solutions (under constant and variable conditions) on their own. By presenting different and unexpected situations the coach promotes creativity in players' actions. On the whole, training centres on tactical decision-making, and in this process specific aspects of position and function of players and team work have an increasing part.

Integrated drills necessitate a balanced training level for quality of exercising. Frequent interruptions resulting from errors have an inhibitory effect. Requirements for initiating complex drills must be carefully controlled, for they determine chiefly the degree of difficulty of the drill tasks. Drill pool summary is shown below.

4.1 Drill Pool

4.1.1 Pass/set/attack: D 208 to D 215
4.1.2 Pass/specific passes/attack
(offensive combinations): D 216 to D 233
4.1.3 Serve/service reception/attack: D 234 toD 246
4.1.4 Serve/service reception/attack sets/attack (offensive combinations): D 247 to D 256
4.1.5 Block/court defence/setting/attack: D 257 to D 327

Court defence (several players co-operating): D 257 to D 262
Combination defence/set: D 263 to D 272
Combination defence/setting/attack: D 273 to D 297
Drill variations in conjunction with block (B-A, A-B, B-ST): D 298 to D 306
Attack coverage/block coverage: D 307 to D 311
Block/defence/setting/attack: D 312 to D 327

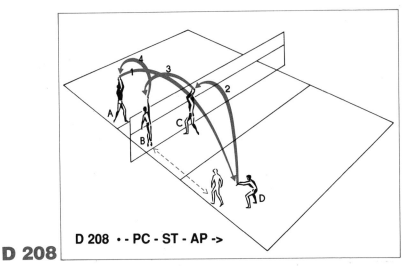

D 208

D 208 · - PC - ST - AP ->

Continuous pass - set - offensive pass. Play passes low (flat) and quickly. Attackers assume ready positions quickly. Preparatory drill for team play in offensive combinations.

Accurate pass - set by back-row setter - spike. Pass to empty area of court; B moves into position to set ball. Start with high passes, then use variations (flat, at shoulder height).

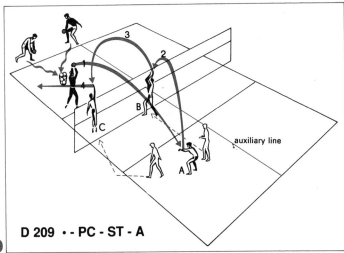

D 209 · - PC - ST - A

D 209

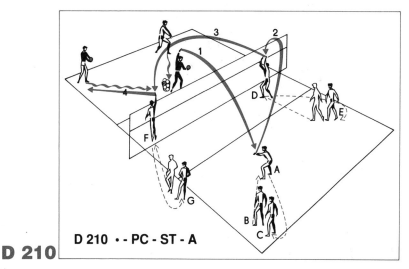

D 210

D 210 • - PC - ST - A

Pass - set - spike under less demanding conditions. Several players change position constantly in one area of play.

Preparation and conclusion of spike after free ball from opponent. Depending upon how the ball is played initially decide about the distribution of tasks and "fluid" execution of the sequence of actions.

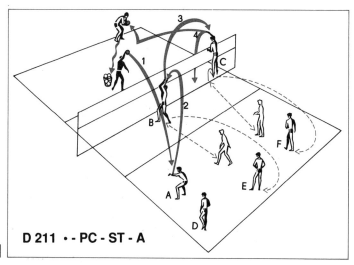

D 211 • - PC - ST - A

D 211

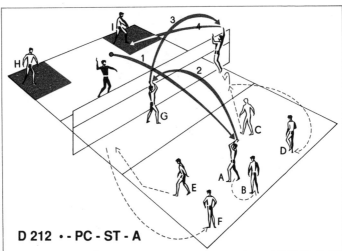

D 212

D 212 • - PC - ST - A

Pass - set - offensive pass/spike. Pass by player A or B to position 3; permanent setter G at position 3 plays high passes to position 2 or 4; offensive pass; then move to offspeed and finally to hard driven spikes toward target. Spike from one position at first, then alternate. Select the pace of the spike so that the target is accurately hit. Use competitive styles. Coach should explain causes of inaccurate spiking by describing how errors result in weak or poor spikes.

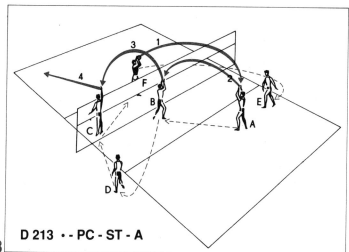

D 213 · - PC - ST - A

D 213

Passes from different positions - set - spike. Preparation for variable offensive formation (forward or back pass); continuous change in ball feeding - pass - set - spike after each action sequence.

Move away quickly from net and form attack after free ball from opponent. Passes by A and B; C, D, E, and F assume setter's role; G, H, and I move quickly away from the net and spike with medium height sets.

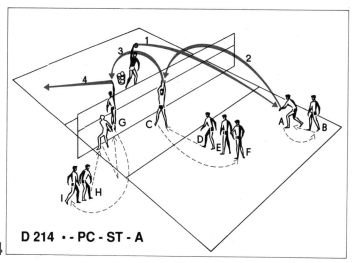

D 214 · - PC - ST - A

D 214

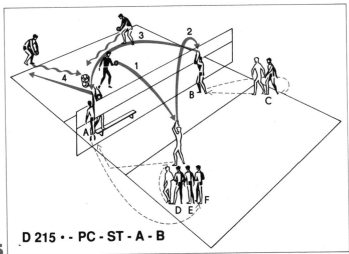

D 215 · · PC - ST - A - B

D 215

Spike past block. Coach blocks inside, outside, or directly on the ball (using punch pads). Depending upon block formation, hit cross-court or down the line or against the block. Do not tip. Play offensively and aggressively.

Spike from attack or quick sets following free ball from opponent. Spike is hit mainly down the line; practise against the block. Practise other elements of variable offensive combinations without obligation to fulfill tactical tasks.

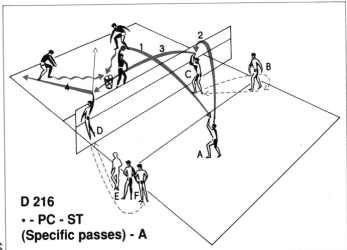

D 216
· - PC - ST
(Specific passes) - A

D 216

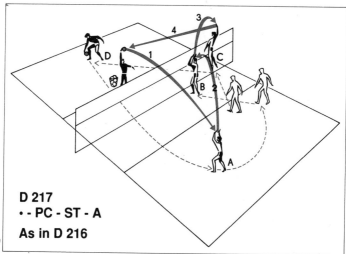

D 217

D 217
• - PC - ST - A
As in D 216

Move away quickly from net and prepare for attack. At the moment the ball is thrown, D, E, and F retreat quickly; direct passes by A. Players C and B set flat balls to position 4; spike. Complete the entire sequence quickly and accurately.

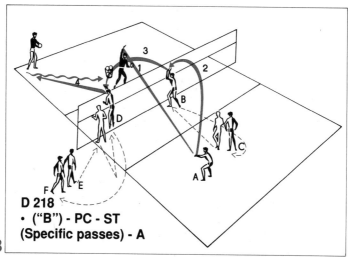

D 218

D 218
• ("B") - PC - ST
(Specific passes) - A

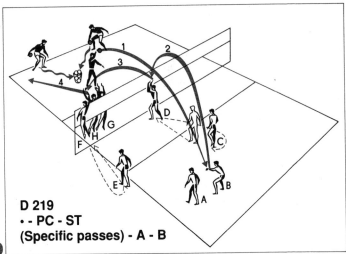

D 219

D 219
• - PC - ST
(Specific passes) - A - B

Attacking block after specific passes. Team play by A and B when passing; flat pass to position 4. Spike at one- or two-player block. Spike on both sides after special passes are made. Hit block.

Offensive combinations after service reception/pass. Two lines of three alternate following each action. Two attackers in the offence. Attacker not involved in hitting must complete the offense by covering the prime attacker.

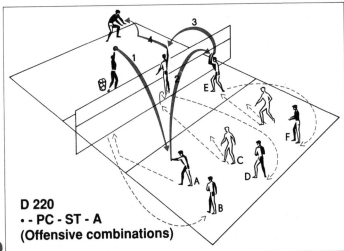

D 220

D 220
• - PC - ST - A
(Offensive combinations)

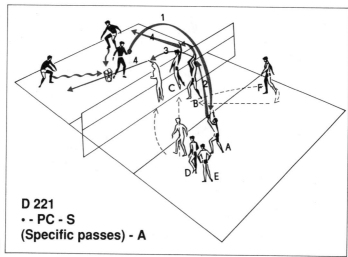

D 221
• - PC - S
(Specific passes) - A

D 221

Vary spike position at centre of net after free ball from opponent.
Offensive preparation for tactically evading block. Conclude attack
aggressively with power driven spikes (straight ahead or with body turn).

Offensive combinations after free balls from opponent. Team play
between a setter and two attackers for offensive combinations: consolidation of spatial and temporal aspects under simplified conditions.

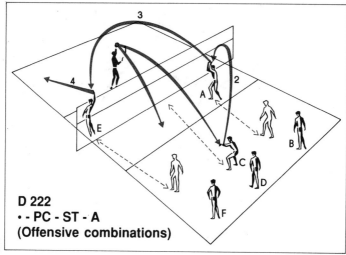

D 222
• - PC - ST - A
(Offensive combinations)

D 222

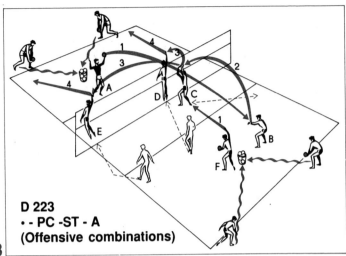

D 223

D 223
• - PC -ST - A
(Offensive combinations)

Formation of offensive combinations after free balls by opponent.
Take turns practising on both sides. "Permanent" setter at net or back-row player sets. Attacker at position 3 begins combination by approaching aggressively expecting set.

Offensive combinations at outside position. Two attackers take up position for offence repeatedly or several attacking pairs alternate repeatedly. Increased physical activity consolidates team play.

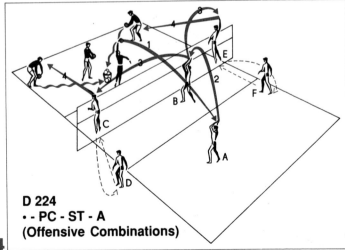

D 224

D 224
• - PC - ST - A
(Offensive Combinations)

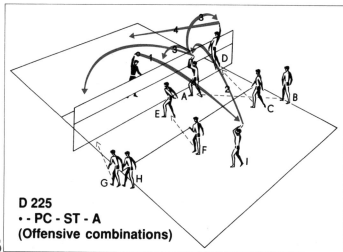

D 225

D 225
• - PC - ST - A
(Offensive combinations)

Offensive combinations with entire offensive line. Team play between a setter and attacker under simplified conditions. All three attackers take up offensive positions and are engaged variably.

Offensive combinations after easy balls from opponent. Front court attackers play several times in a row. After spike has been completed, resume starting position again. Setters "feed" passes variably.

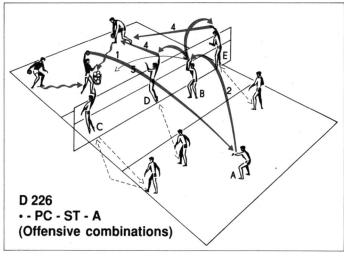

D 226

D 226
• - PC - ST - A
(Offensive combinations)

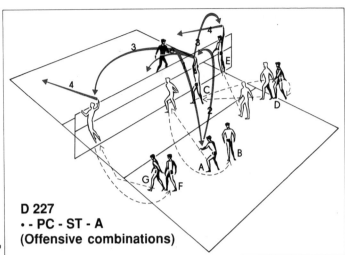

D 227
• - PC - ST - A
(Offensive combinations)

D 227

Offensive combinations after easy balls from opponent. Team play between back-row setter and three attackers. Consolidation of spatial/temporal co-ordination. Several groups of four alternate practising repeatedly.

Learning to choose between several possible combinations. Ball is played to back-row setter. Team play by setter with two attackers. C "pulls" or leads the combination by going in front of or behind the back-row setter; B crosses over or assumes centre hitting position by hitting a "metre ball."

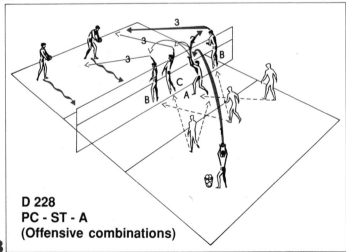

D 228
PC - ST - A
(Offensive combinations)

D 228

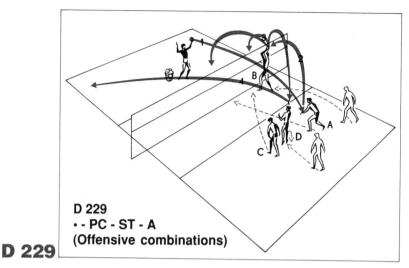

D 229
• - PC - ST - A
(Offensive combinations)

D 229

Inclusion of attack from backcourt in offensive combinations. Easy ball from opponent - accurate pass. A and C take up positions for offensive combination. Setter alternately passes to them and also D (periodically) in backcourt.

Conclude offensive combinations with targeted spikes. Even in offensive combinations players must reckon with playing against a block. It is therefore incorrect to attack blindly and too hard.

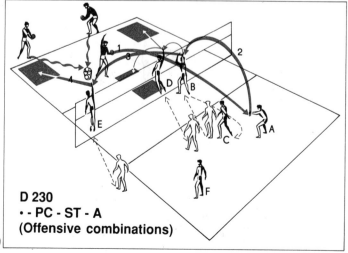

D 230
• - PC - ST - A
(Offensive combinations)

D 230

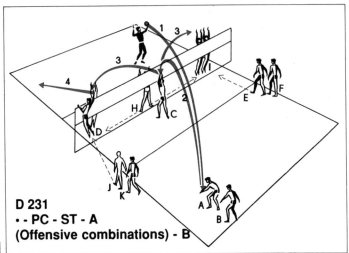

D 231
• - PC - ST - A
(Offensive combinations) - B

D 231

Spike against two-player block after easy ball from opponent. Pass
to position 3. Vary set by setting forward or back (shoulder height to flat).
Spike against two-player block. Middle blocker closes the block.

Fake attack - jump pass - spike. Ball is thrown. A plays direct pass to
position 4; B completes action as far as swinging arm back (as in offence),
then turns towards position 3 and makes jump pass to C, who spikes the
ball. On occasion B may spike directly.

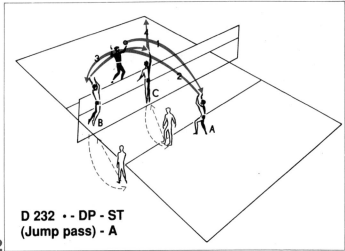

D 232 • - DP - ST
(Jump pass) - A

D 232

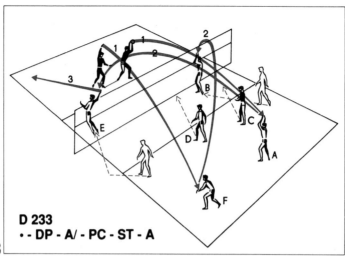

D 233
• - DP - A/ - PC - ST - A

D 233

Direct pass - attack or offensive combination with entire offensive line. Formation of offensive combination with entire frontcourt line or a after signal by E who plays direct set pass immediately. Cover attacker when practising with block. Set direct passes to outside positions.

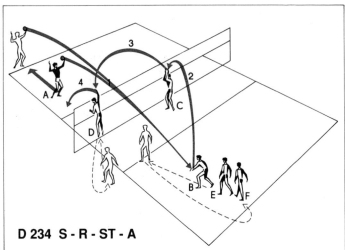

D 234

D 234 S - R - ST - A

Service reception - set - spike under simplified conditions. When practising, always remember that the way an action is executed determines the conditions for the next player.

Combine service reception with set. Use easy serves; pass serve in collaboration with next player. In cases of doubt call out to make known who receives the ball.

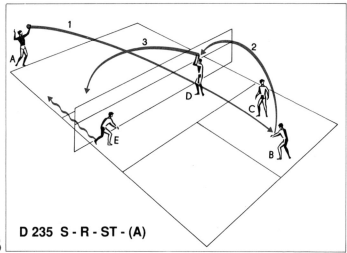

D 235

D 235 S - R - ST - (A)

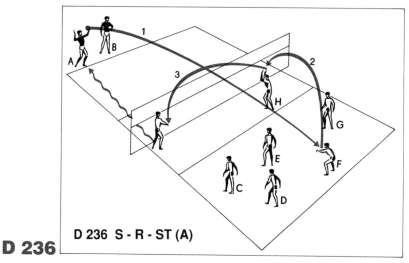

D 236 S - R - ST (A)

D 236

Service reception with five-player line - set. Players agree who will receive the serve and make the pass to position 2 at net. Change after approximately 5 minutes. Make sure that pace is steady.

Passing serve in pairs - set - spike. Team play between frontcourt/ backcourt players when receiving serves. Pairs change frequently. After receiving player D runs forward to simulate coverage.

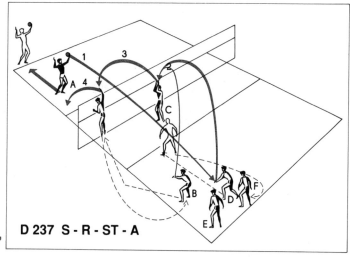

D 237 S - R - ST - A

D 237

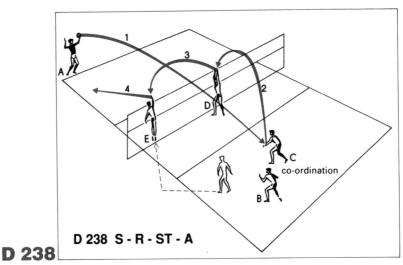

D 238 S - R - ST - A

D 238

Spike with high or quick set depending upon quality of service reception. Watch the receiving player carefully and decide whether you can attack effectively from a fast, low pass played to you by the setter.

Formation of offence after light serves. Players C and E simulate attack coverage; team play for actions in sequence "recovery - set-up - spike" and adapt to continue play.

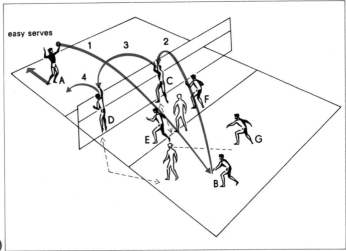

D 239

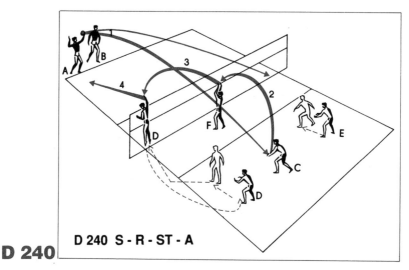

D 240

D 240 S - R - ST - A

Service reception - set - spike. Set to positions 2 or 4; attackers do not receive. Encourages team play co-ordination.

Formation and conclusion of offence after opponents' serve. Player D receives serve accurately; high pass to attacker at position 4; line attack; server A digs attack. Emphasis on motor accuracy by server, receiver and attacker. Hit easy serves at first.

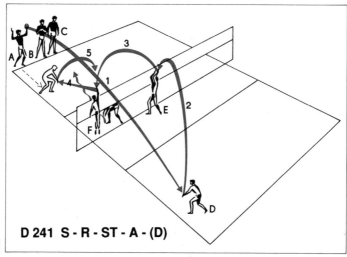

D 241 S - R - ST - A - (D)

D 241

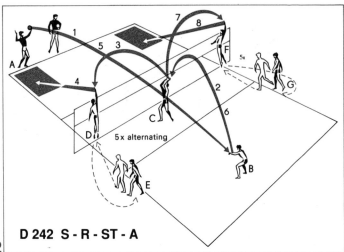

D 242

D 242 S - R - ST - A

Placeded spikes from high passes after recovery of serve. From position 3 alternate sets to positions 2 and 4. Spike down line toward target. Jump to maximum height. Hit long and do not pull the ball down by dropping elbow.

Changing difficulty of reception - regular offensive formation. Depending upon the serve (alternate between easy and difficult), aim for maximum accuracy when passing serve. It is imperative to ensure uninterrupted flow of action by passing the serve well.

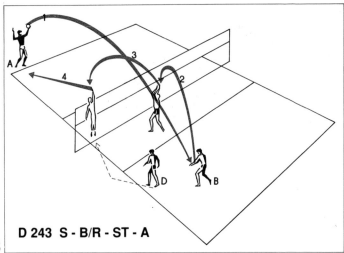

D 243 S - B/R - ST - A

D 243

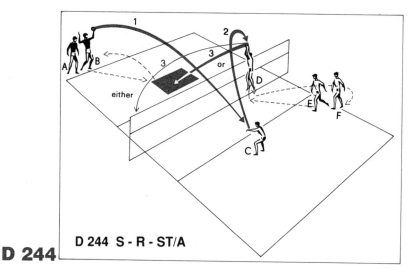

D 244   D 244 S - R - ST/A

Play unexpectedly to opponent Back-row player, after receiving pass from C (easy serves), plays jump set to position 4 or fakes to play the ball (balls close to net) to target area in opponents' court.

Cover attack after service reception. Service reception with three-player line. Play blocked ball or ball thrown directly to position 3. Variation: after recovery, form a new attack immediately.

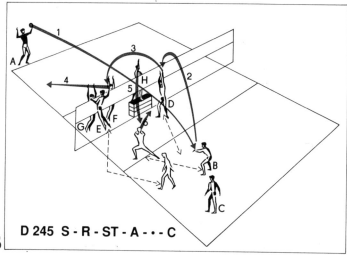

D 245   D 245 S - R - ST - A - · · C

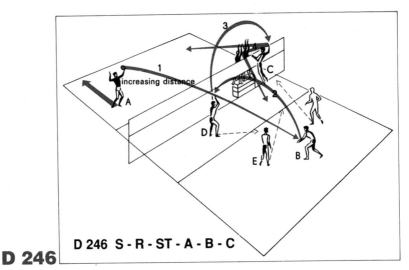

D 246   D 246 S - R - ST - A - B - C

Passing of serve - set - spike and cover. Players are prepared for continuting action sequence. They cover the attack and play block rebound high enough for another attack build-up.

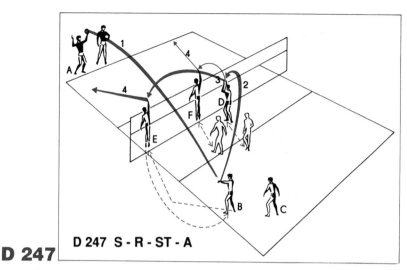

D 247

D 247 S - R - ST - A

Offensive combinations with two attackers after passing of serve.
Passing of serve in pairs; E and F are prepared to attack. Attackers play
variably using specific passes.

Performing offensive combinations after service reception. Easy
serves. B passes serve; F, D, and E attack combination sets by C.
Emphasize accurate service reception.

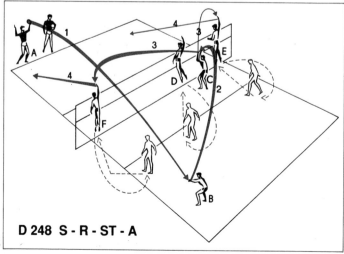

D 248

D 248 S - R - ST - A

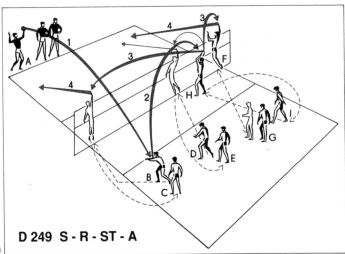

D 249

D 249 S - R - ST - A

Service reception - offensive combinations. Developing spatial and temporal co-ordination (court sense and timing). With the aid of a signal system call in advance the planned offensive combinations.

Offensive combinations with two attackers after passing of serve. Team play between D and E with F (setter) in the offensive combination ("rising" ball, position 3, "metre ball", position 2).

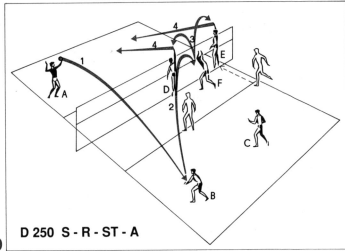

D 250

D 250 S - R - ST - A

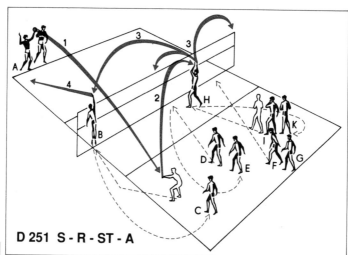

D 251

D 251 S - R - ST - A

Co-ordination between passing of serve - set - spike. Hit easy serves; pass serve to back-row setter's area (between positions 2 and 3); set to one of the attackers. Spike with and without block. Set target tasks.

Offensive combinations against (single-player) block after service reception. Accurate passing of the serve is essential for using offensive combinations. Disrupt block by disguising the set as much as possible.

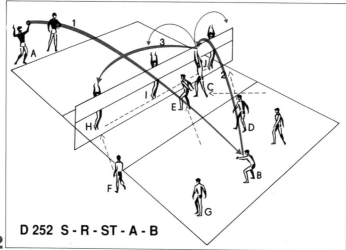

D 252

D 252 S - R - ST - A - B

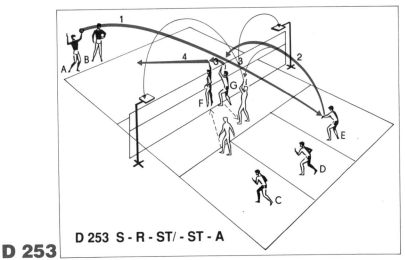

D 253

D 253 S - R - ST/ - ST - A

Choosing type of set based on reception accuracy. Depending upon the accuracy of reception, set ball high forward or back. Try to attack by striking ball at the highest point of its trajectory.

Service reception - set - spike. Five-player reception, back-row player sets. Attack is spread across entire frontcourt attackers. Variation: after first action sequence throw ball in for a first-pass attack.

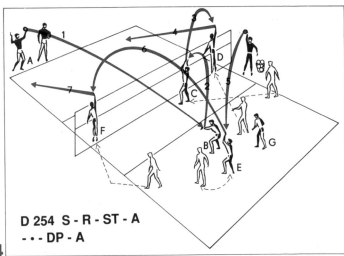

D 254 S - R - ST - A
- • - DP - A

D 254

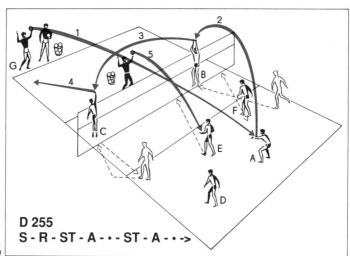

D 255

D 255
S - R - ST - A - • • ST - A - • ->

Four consecutive offensive combinations. First offensive combination after passing of serve, then throw three easy balls to one of the backcourt players. Passes and offensive combinations using the entire frontcourt line.

Service reception and attack is followed by next series of actions.
Two successive attacks are performed based on various defensive plays (passing of serve, defence - coverage). Do not play with undue haste.

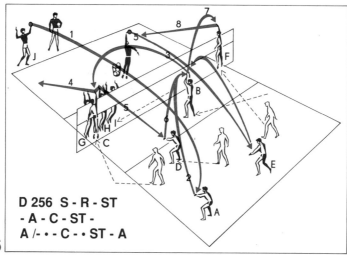

D 256 S - R - ST
- A - C - ST -
A /- • • C - • ST - A

D 256

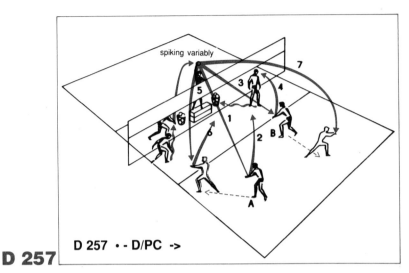

D 257 | D 257 · - D/PC ->

Training of Japanese court defence. A and B alternate receiving difficult balls, either hit or thrown by coach. Practise for approximately one minute, then switch. Emphasize aggressive defence.

Defensive training movement to ball. Variation of "Japanese" court defence. Coach hits balls so that centre player (B) must move to the left and right, whereas players A and C take hits going short and toward the middle.

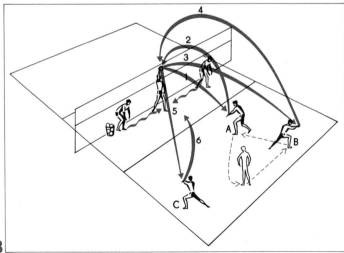

D 258

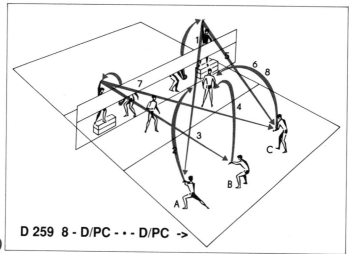

D 259 8 - D/PC - · - D/PC ->

D 259

Defence in threes with variable spike direction. Variation of "Japanese" court defence drill. Increased demands on concentration and ability to focus on ball coming from different direction; intensive physical training from rapid exercise pace.

Attack from backcourt (long distance balls) and defence. Improving of spiking under difficult conditions (jumping to maximum height, arm stretched, no pulling down of ball). Try to defend every ball.

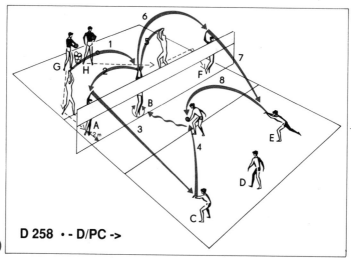

D 258 · - D/PC ->

D 260

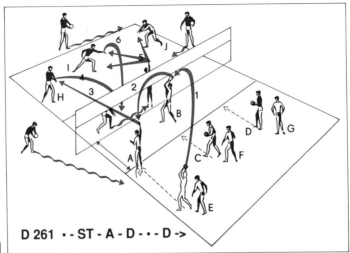

D 261 · - ST - A - D - · · - D ->

D 261

Digging spikes from backcourt and expecting another ball immediately after. Balls are fed so as to train players ability to react and change defensive positions quickly. Aim for accurate defensive passing.

Continuous defense of spikes. Throw in new ball (to A) whenever defensive faults are made. Be mobile in defense and watch the attackers. Communicate and once movement toward ball has been initiated, complete the play. (A sets ball for second ball attack from positions 2 and 4.)

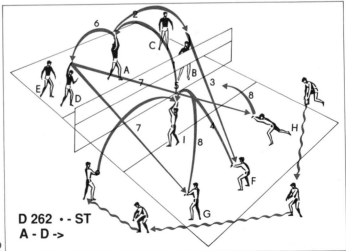

D 262 · - ST
A - D ->

D 262

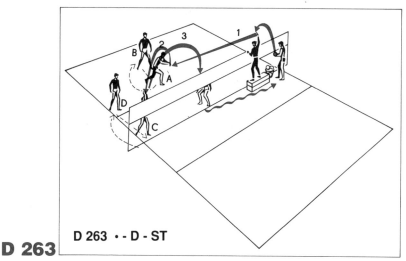

D 263

D 263 · - D - ST

Set after court defence. Two or three players alternate practising continuously. Try to anticipate where inaccurate digs will fall and move toward correct playing position in good time. Coach observes attentively and makes players correct play position.

Digging of line attacks and sets by back-row player. Remain deep during defence. Crouch down, bring body behind the ball, while still facing play. Do not "run forwards" for court defence until ball is approaching.

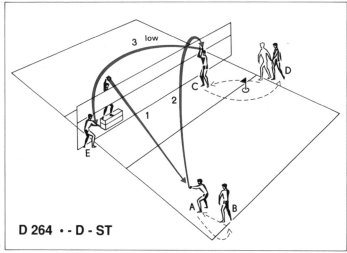

D 264

D 264 · - D - ST

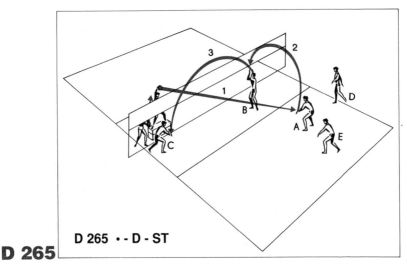

D 265 · - D - ST

D 265

Setting balls bumped in a high trajectory to the net. Practise in series (approximately 10 times) or continuous change after each play. Pace should allow proper motor execution.

Team play on defensive line (combination defence - set from centre of court). New ball is thrown in or hit by coach when faults are made. Setter (C) should set high to position 4. Emphasize carrying out actions while moving.

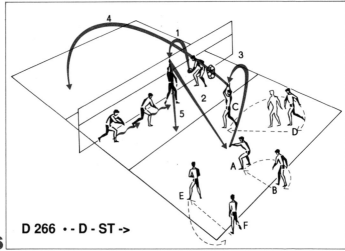

D 266 · - D - ST ->

D 266

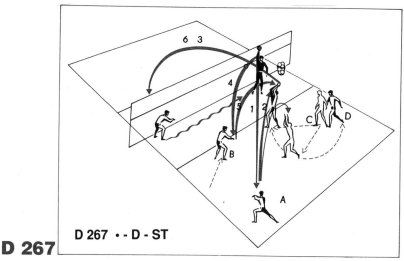

D 267 · - D - ST

D 267

Combine defence with set. Maximize defensive effort. Watch other players carefully and, in the event of inaccurate plays, change path taken towards playing position. Do not "rush" towards the ball. Emphasize good high sets to position 4.

Combine court defence with set. Two players each dig moderately driven shots. Permanent front-row setter sets. Variation: set back to position 2 and repeat attack.

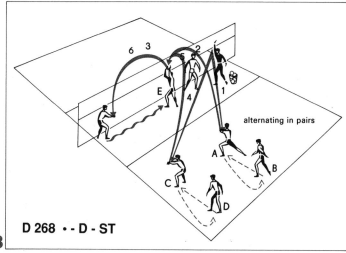

D 268 · - D - ST

D 268

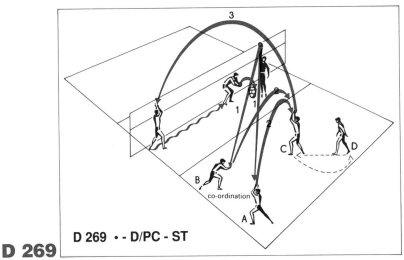

D 269

D 269 · - D/PC - ST

Combine defence with set from back court. Dig power driven spikes safely to centre court; high diagonal passes to position 4. Use attackers as setters (player C).

Combine defence of attack with set. Dig attack to position 3 and set forward and overhead backwards. Do not lunge diagonally forwards when playing defence. Remain deep and go forwards and inside from outside.

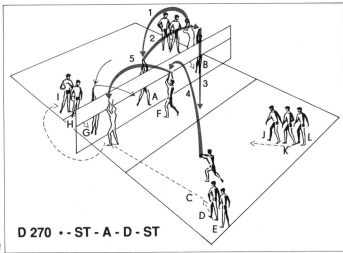

D 270 · - ST - A - D - ST

D 270

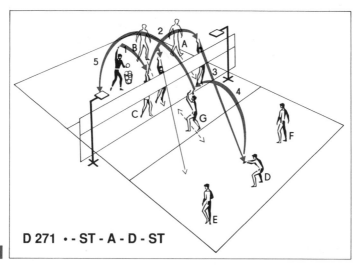

D 271

D 271 · - ST - A - D - ST

Defence in threes - set to target. Long, deep spikes into backcourt; bump to position 3; set (diagonal passes to position 4).After defence into front court, player plays parallel passes overhead backwards.

Accurate digging of attack and set to target. Try to dig all balls with two-handed bump. Play safe, high passes. Continuous practising helps improve recovery and set-up.

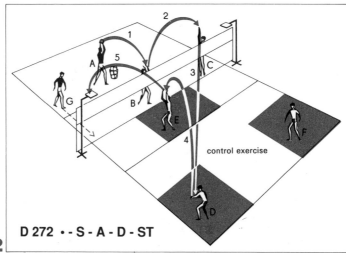

control exercise

D 272

D 272 · - S - A - D - ST

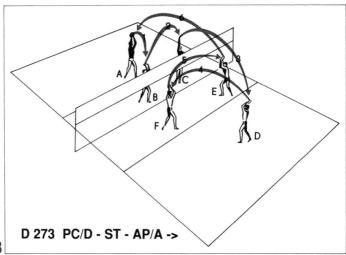

D 273

D 273 PC/D - ST - AP/A ->

Attack pass during fluid "3 on 3" exercising. Different variations of attack passes are played in conjunction with preceding play actions (prepare team-work for formation and conclusion of attack).

Two spikes in a row based on different preparation for attacks. Setter plays different passes (high, outside, inside, quick, etc.). Attackers spike, adapting quickly to new situation.

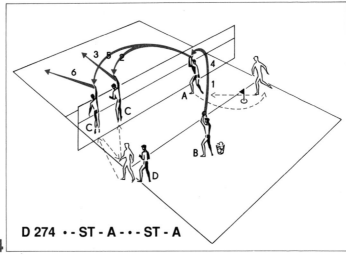

D 274 ·· ST - A -·· ST - A

D 274

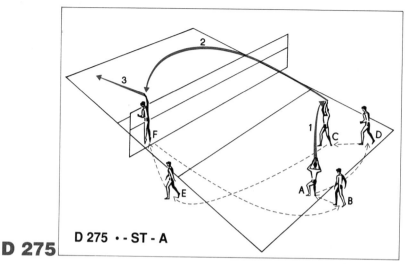

D 275   D 275 · - ST - A

Set from backcourt and spiking. Specific exercise for attackers. Preparation for setting poorly passed ball diagonally and attacking the set.

Set - spike following different predetermined actions. Standard high pass to outside under simplified conditions. Spike high set. Practise delaying approach, then move quickly to spike.

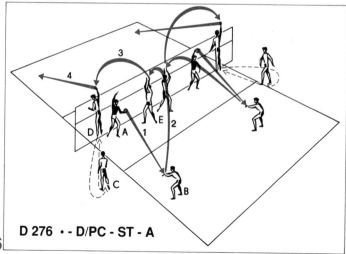

D 276   D 276 · - D/PC - ST - A

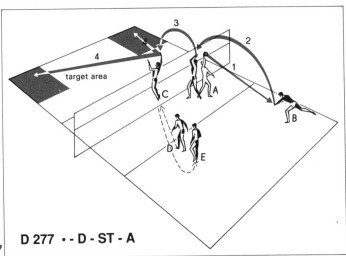

D 277   D 277 · - D - ST - A

Defence - set - spike. Player A hits the ball to player B, who digs and plays the pass himself; player A sets pass. Players C, D, and E assume offensive positions and hit in the direction of approach or across body to targets in deep corners.

Combine defence - set - spike. Long diagonal spike; correct position for defensive player's spike from position 4; also spike so that defensive players must cover part of position 6 as well. Conduct as continuous drill with experienced players.

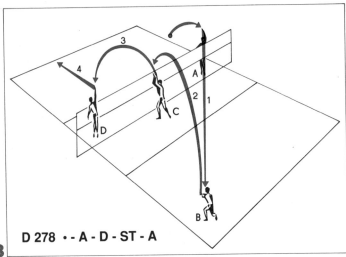

D 278   D 278 · - A - D - ST - A

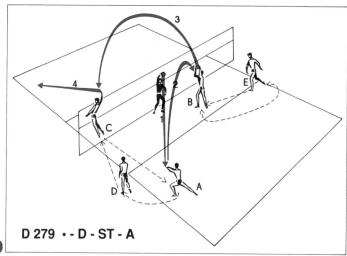

D 279

D 279 · - D - ST - A

Combine defence - set and spike. Alternate hitters or have player attack two to three times in a row. Move away from net quickly and assume ready position.

Defence - set - attack with three groups of three. Improve the movement sequences within the action sequence; groups change after approximately 5 to 10 actions per player. Emphasize quality of play.

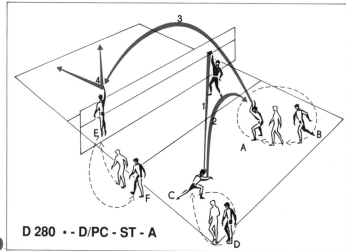

D 280

D 280 · - D/PC - ST - A

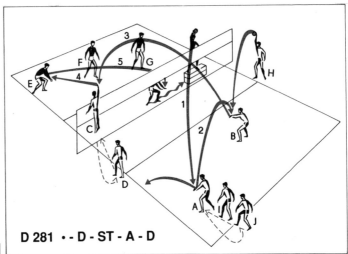

D 281 · - D - ST - A - D

D 281

Spike from diagonal passes after weak defence. Defending power driven spikes to position 5. High diagonal passes or bump pass to position 4 - spike. After defence error, throw in new ball to player B for set.

Continuous practise "spike - defence - set." Hit controlled spikes directly towards the defensive player. Have 2 groups of 3 players on each half. With experienced players, play "3 on 3," alternating 5 minutes of play with 5 minutes of rest.

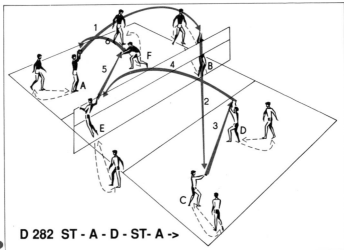

D 282 ST - A - D - ST- A ->

D 282

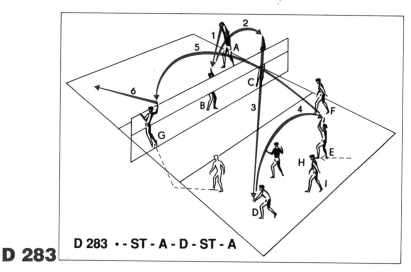

D 283

D 283 • - ST - A - D - ST - A

Defence without block - attack set from backcourt. After deciding on defending without a block, attack is formed according to the quality of the dug ball.

Defensive spikes from backcourt and forming own attack. Frontcourt block line moves quickly away from net during attack. Setter from backcourt moves to setting position. Proceed quickly from defence to attack and back again.

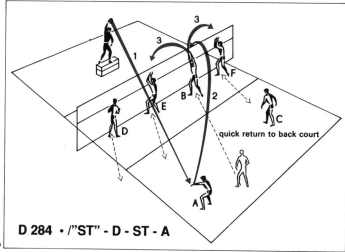

quick return to back court

D 284

D 284 • /"ST" - D - ST - A

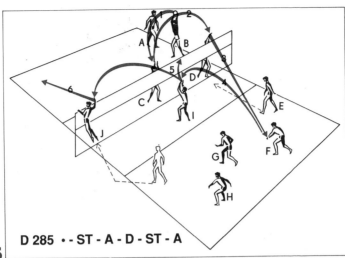

D 285 · - ST - A - D - ST - A

D 285

Defence without block and form attack via frontcourt setter. Defence with five-player formations; set either forward or back. Simply pass ball to the nearest attacker, then opt for "long distance" play.

Set pass or regular attack formation following easy balls from opponent. A, E, and F move quickly from ready block position and decide whether first pass attack is feasible, or whether A, E and F should attack from second pass.

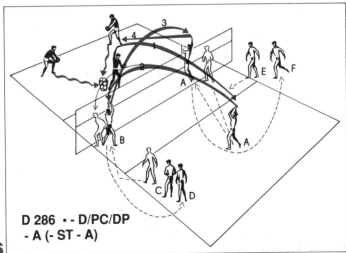

D 286 · - D/PC/DP
- A (- ST - A)

D 286

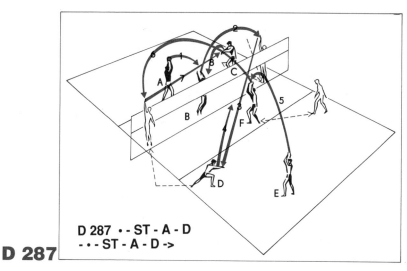

D 287

D 287 • - ST - A - D
- • - ST - A - D ->

Transition switching from court defence to counter attack. After attack move away quickly from the net and assume ready position to defend opponents' attack. Following defence, prepare quickly for attack.

Defence and prepare immediately for attack. Tip or offspeed from box; pass to position 2; complete attack quickly with spike (practise at positions 3 and 4); player C tosses to D, who sets to positions 3 or 4.

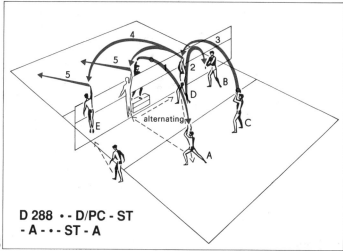

D 288

D 288 • - D/PC - ST
- A - • - ST - A

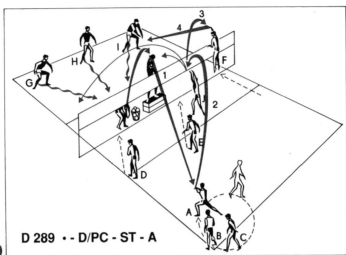

D 289

D 289 · - D/PC - ST - A

Spike attack sets after easy balls from opponent. Easy passes to setter; set quick to middle or outside; or back to position 2 to shoulder height ("metre ball"); spike mainly down line. Practise also against a block.

Defence - pass - set-up - spike for one player. Player A makes three consecutive plays with the ball: (1) digs ball hit by C; (2) sets ball from B; (3) attacks set from C. Extra players ensure rapid progression of exercise.

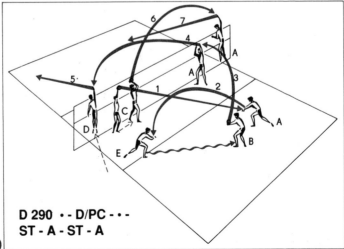

D 290

D 290 · - D/PC - · -
ST - A - ST - A

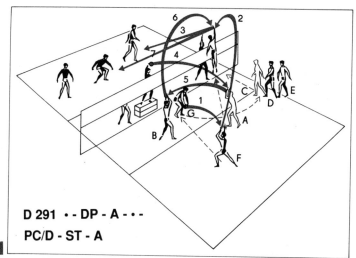

D 291 · - DP - A - · -
PC/D - ST - A

D 291

After spike from diagonal pass adapt quickly to new situation and perform accurate court pass. Player A attacks from a pass received from F and returns quickly; court pass to B who sets up a high pass for C, etc.

Two consecutive spikes from different passes. Repeated spiking. On second play attacker receives a diagonal set from backcourt (player F). Variation: play a fake pass if there is a block, and attack hard with lack of block.

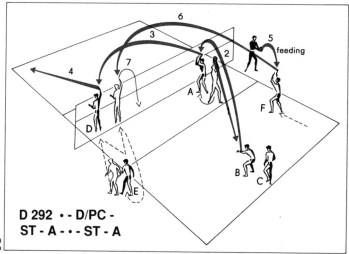

D 292 · - D/PC -
ST - A - · - ST - A

D 292

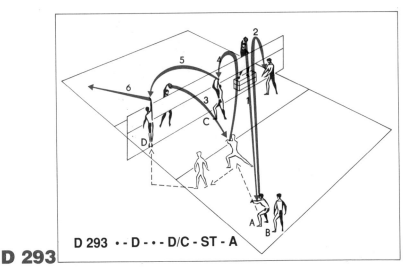

D 293

D 293 · - D - · · D/C - ST - A

Several plays in quick succession (D, PC, A). Improve different structures of movements. First dig deep cross-court, then sharp cross-court. Complete each action well before proceeding to the next one.

Alternate between defence and attack. Recover offspeeds hit from box so that a direct spike is possible or a set to position 4.

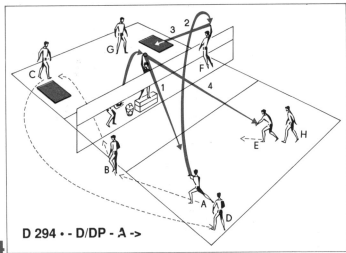

D 294

D 294 · - D/DP - A ->

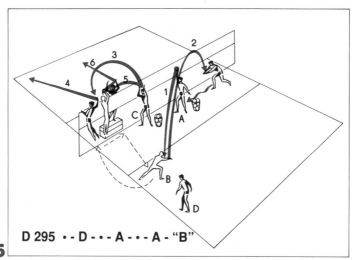

D 295 · - D - · · - A - · · · - A - "B"

D 295

Dig and spike twice in rapid succession. Ball dug across sharp cross-court; move to spike from position 4. Then run up one step, inside hit, a quick set against one- or two-player block.

Direct spike. Preparation for alternative actions following free balls from opponent (pass to setter or directly to hitter). Emphasis in exercise is placed on execution of the direct pass.

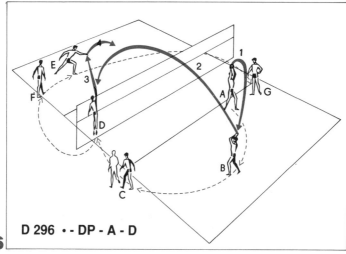

D 296 · - DP - A - D

D 296

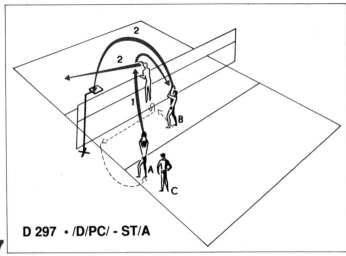

D 297

D 297 · /D/PC/ - ST/A

Set or spike from direct pass. On basis of flight path of the ball, player B decides whether to spike immediately (feint pass, spike) or to set a high pass.

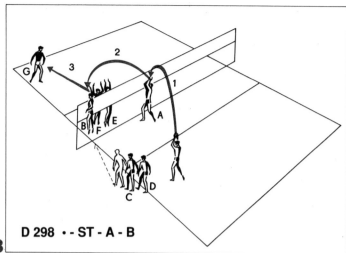

D 298 · - ST - A - B

D 298

Observe two-player block when spiking. Spike from position 4 to defensive players at position 1. If block does not cover line, drive spike down along the line. If block covers the ball, offspeed the ball over the block.

Spike against block. Set-up across moderate distance. Attacker concentrates on block and acts according to demands described in D 129.

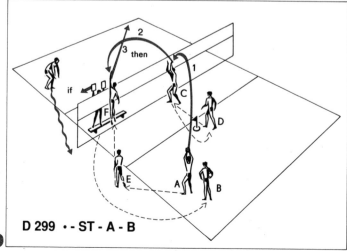

D 299 · - ST - A - B

D 299

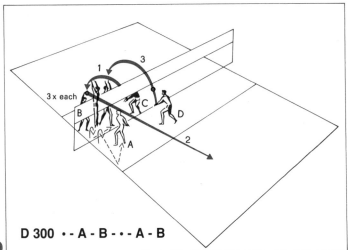

D 300 · - A - B - · - A - B

D 300

Continuous change between spike and blocking. Player B spikes. Player A forms a single-player block. New ball is fed to A who has less time to prepare for attack, etc. After blocking and spiking, be prepared immediately for next play.

Rapid alternation between block - spike. B blocks ball, moves back and then spikes at position 4. Block and offensive plays in rapid alternation. The drill places high demands on technical and co-ordination execution as well as the physical exertion.

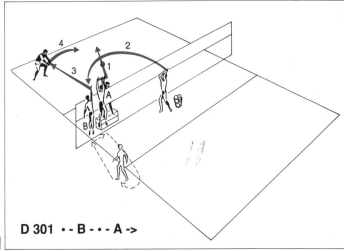

D 301 · - B - · - A ->

D 301

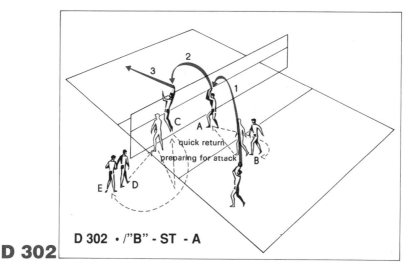

D 302 • /"B" - ST - A

D 302

Assume offensive position immediately after block. Spike after blocking; block jump when ball is passed; after landing move quickly away from the net and spike after complete run-up.

Different actions to follow simulated block jumps. Variant 1: block - spike; Variant 2: block - recovery/pass. Watch frontcourt players as you land and carry on smoothly with succeeding play. Balls are fed variably.

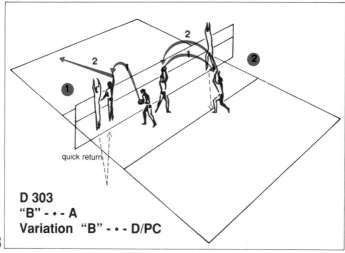

D 303
"B" - • - A
Variation "B" - • - D/PC

D 303

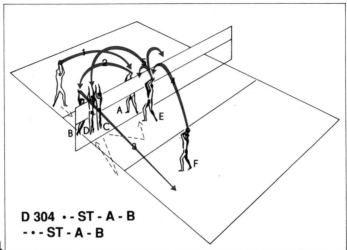

D 304 · - ST - A - B
- · - ST - A - B

D 304

Spike - block in rapid succession. B spikes past two-man block; C and D move quickly away from the net after block and assume offensive positions. A and B block their respective attackers.

Blocking before setting. The block players jump as ball leaves passer's hands; land ready for next action as you watch passer. Ball is set to position 4. Change after every or after every 2 to 3 plays.

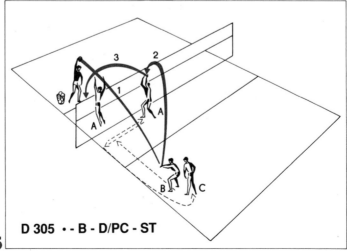

D 305 · - B - D/PC - ST

D 305

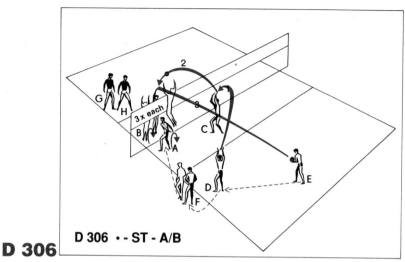

D 306

D 306 · - ST - A/B

Pass close to opponent at net. Normal set by C or overset to opponent. B must change quickly to offence with limited preparation time if ball overset. A moves to block or spikes as usual.

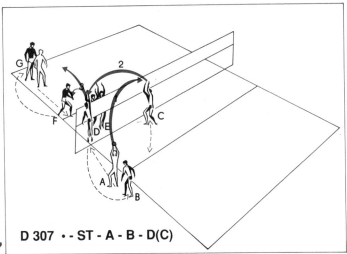

D 307   D 307 • - ST - A - B - D(C)

Backcourt player covers. Depending upon type of attack and block, play defence correctly or cover block. Variation: block - fake pass-covering in position 2; no block - line attack - defending player covers back court

Recover ball and cover. A digs spike; B oversets; C stimulates block rebound, which A must dig. A moves back to play another court defence; 3 to 5 repetitions.

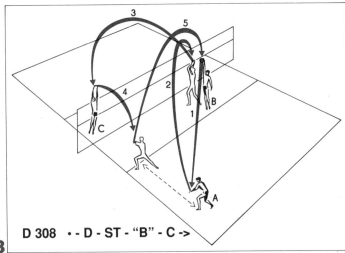

          D 308 • - D - ST - "B" - C ->

D 308

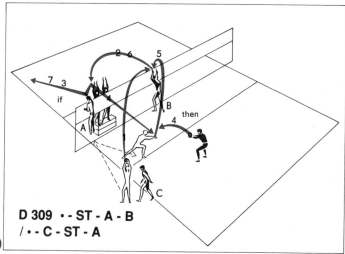

D 309

D 309 ·-ST-A-B
/·-C-ST-A

Spike at two-player block - coverage and repeated spike. If the ball rebounds off the block, cover your own position and repeat attack. If necessary, new ball is thrown. Try to hit block so that you can attack again.

Cover quickly after spike. Spike at two-man block, hit into block and recover ball back to setter or, if hit pass the block, move back and receive short cross-court hit. While landing observe the next ball.

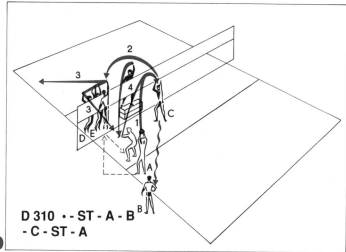

D 310

D 310 ·-ST-A-B
-C-ST-A

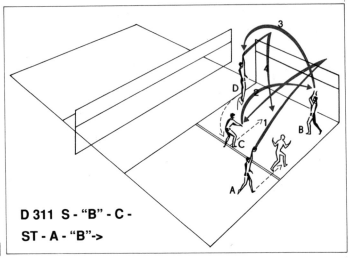

D 311

D 311 S - "B" - C -
ST - A - "B"->

Attack formation after attack coverage for rebounds on wall. A and C cover; B sets (approximately 2 metres away from wall). D hits the ball against the wall (lob, feint). Repeat three to five times, then rotate to next position.

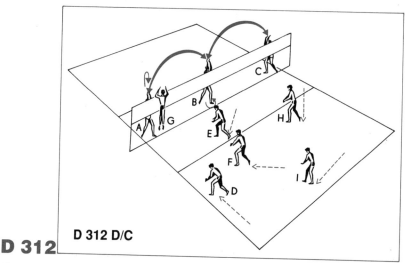

D 312 D 312 D/C

Simulation of defensive formation. Single-player block (two-player block) is formed wherever intermediate play is made. All other players run quickly to their defensive areas. Explain correct positional play slowly.

Recovery of line attack and back pass to blocker for spike. Team assistant attacks against single-player block; B digs to frontcourt. Blocker A moves away from the net and spikes with back pass from C.

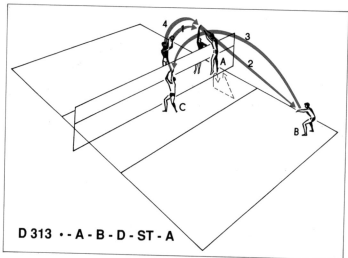

D 313 D 313 · · A - B - D - ST - A

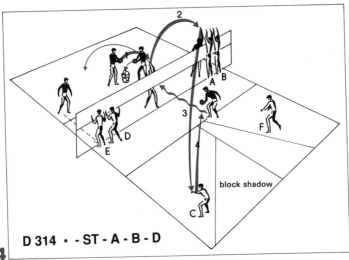

D 314   D 314 • - ST - A - B - D

Team play block - recovery. Work on having tight block; do not form two single-player blocks. Do not build offensive block, but instead cover an area of the court, a zone block. Defensive players should orient themselves around block (outside of block shadow).

Building up counter-attack after block/recovery. C and B jump to block, change quickly, and ready themselves to set or to attack. Set to position 4 - attack. Change positions after 5 series.

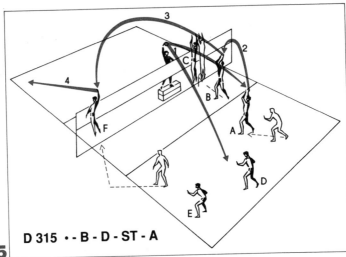

D 315 • - B - D - ST - A

D 315

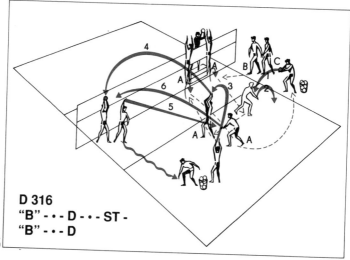

D 316

D 316
"B" - · - D - · · - ST -
"B" - · · - D

Rapid sequence of plays (for one player). Player A blocks, recovers short tossed ball, blocks, plays ball thrown in high, sets high diagonal pass, and concludes with immediate defence of ball hit from position 4.

Play easy serves or tips immediately as first pass attack. Tip or offspeed over two-man block. Backcourt player takes up block cover, makes direct pass to position 2. Variation: set up high passes to position 4 (E, F, G).

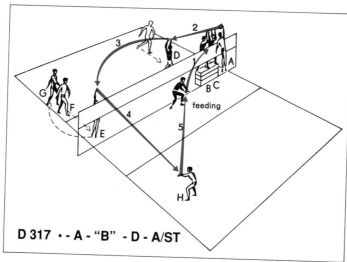

D 317 · - A - "B" - D - A/ST

D 317

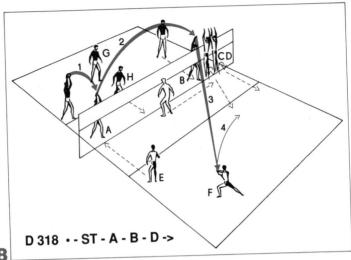

D 318 · - ST - A - B - D -›

D 318

Switching from block/court defence to counter-attack. Two-player block against spikes from position 4. Dig ball to frontcourt (position 2/3). Players E, C, and D attack.

Move from block quickly and prepare for set. A and B form a two-player block against spikes from position 4. Dig to frontcourt between positions 2 and 3 (use four-player defensive line). Blocker in best position sets a pass to position 4.

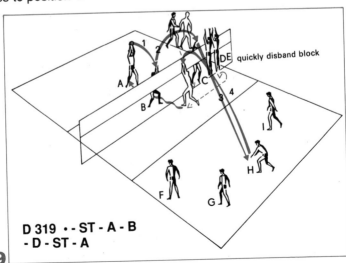

D 319 · - ST - A - B
- D - ST - A

D 319

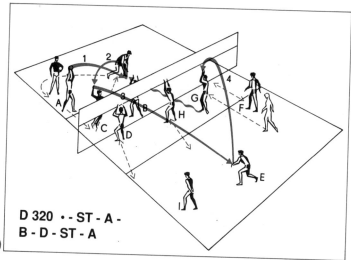

D 320

D 320 ・- ST - A -
B - D - ST - A

Switching from block/recovery to counter-attack (combinations).
Vary spike from all court positions; blocker moves away from net after
spike. Passer is ready to attack as back-row setter; one of the front line
players prepares himself to play.

Block - recovery with complete six. Spike against two-player block
(offensive position known) - defence according to tactical system to be
used by coach (i.e., players take up their respective positions, block is
covered by back court player, etc.).

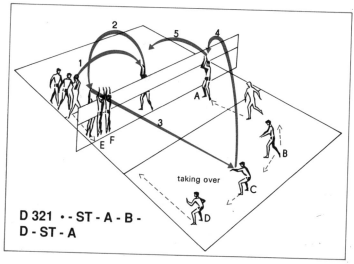

D 321 ・- ST - A - B -
D - ST - A

D 321

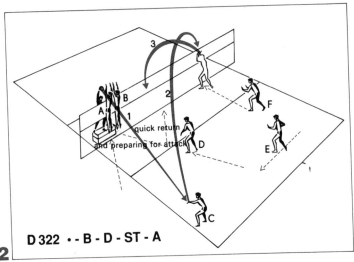

D 322 · - B - D - ST - A

D 322

Block - defence - counter-attack. Team play among defensive players (6 players playing up) with offensive position already known.

Attack formation after free balls from opponent. When ball is played frontcourt players jump to form single-player block and run immediately to attack line. B moves from backcourt for set (A sets when B passes; when F passes decide whether A or B sets forward). Set high passes or form combination attacks.

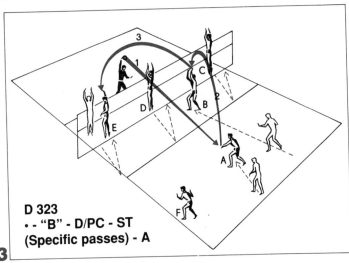

D 323
· - "B" - D/PC - ST
(Specific passes) - A

D 323

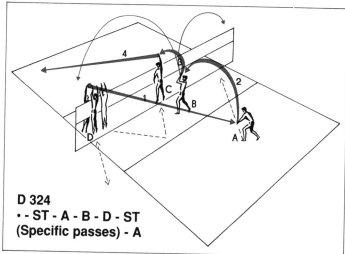

D 324

D 324
• - ST - A - B - D - ST
(Specific passes) - A

Rapid transition from recovery to counter-attack. Two-player block and defence of short, diagonal spike (easy, controlled spikes). Afterwards assume offensive position. Vary spikes and also use offensive combinations.

Set up return spike quickly after three-player block. Spikes to player A or F, with row of frontcourt players jumping to form three-man block. B takes up position as setter and sets pass to a ready attacker.

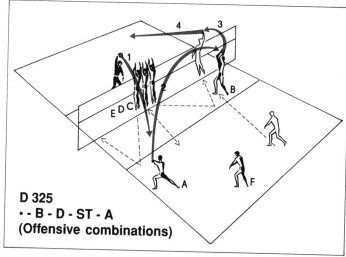

D 325

D 325
• - B - D - ST - A
(Offensive combinations)

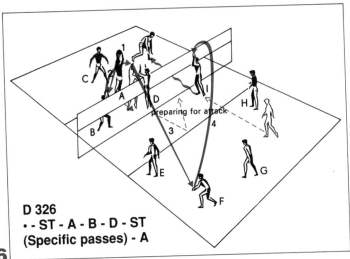

D 326

D 326
• - ST - A - B - D - ST
(Specific passes) - A

Recovery and return spike after single-player block at position 3.
Move away from the net after single-player block and assume offensive
position. Setter moves from court to setting position. Outside frontcourt
players cover single-player block.

Block - recovery - formation of counter-attack. Block against high
spikes - position for attack; team play among defensive line; formation for
counter-attack.

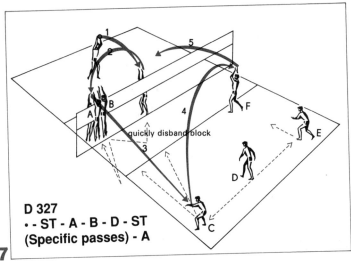

D 327
• - ST - A - B - D - ST
(Specific passes) - A

D 327

5 Game Simulation and Scrimmage on Smaller Courts

The game simulation and scrimmaging on a reduced court size are more complex forms of exercise. Here, too, a number of elements are applied in the sequence of play, but the various situations and phases of play occur in far less controlled manner and in different succession. Training focusses mainly on teaching players to make a constant transition between defence and offence under constantly changing conditions. Players have to apply their skills, with increasing demands made on their athletic ability.

These forms of practice can be varied quite readily in training and can be influenced externally (i.e., by feeding a ball) despite the unpredictability of the play process. The external control by the coach is concerned primarily with increasing physical and tactical demands. The smaller court games are included primarily to familiarize players with competitive conditions (suitable for all age groups). They can be fitted well to players' skill levels by altering the dimensions of the court and by establishing additional rules. Training games (practice games, training games similar to matches) are the most advanced level of technical and tactical training as a play form. From the point of view of methodology and content, competitive forms (Chapter 7) are used in training with specific objectives (not victory, but rather tactical objectives).

The transition to these forms of practice occurs by the so-called "one-sided play" (serve remains with one team; the other team is always defensive; break-up after counter-attack). Drills for Complexes I and II may, in principle, be included here.

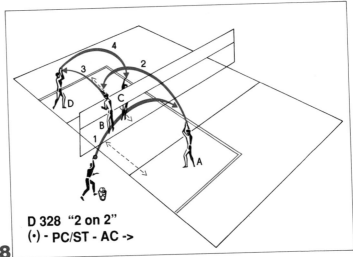

D 328 "2 on 2"
(•) - PC/ST - AC ->

D 328

"2 on 2" on smaller court. "Normal" play (underarm serve) or coach throws in balls after interruptions in play. Decide whether a set pass is possible or normal offensive formation. Use offensive sets, offspeeds, and tips.

"6 on 6" (pass, set-up, offensive pass). Ball is played from centre; use different types of sets. Variation: after each offensive pass rotate smoothly to the next position.

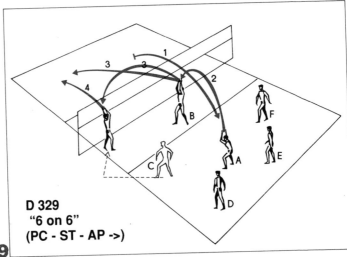

D 329
"6 on 6"
(PC - ST - AP ->)

D 329

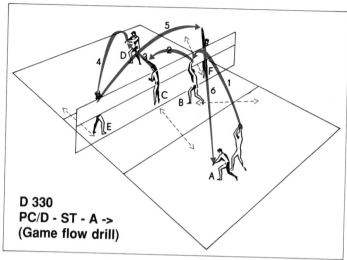

D 330
PC/D - ST - A ->
(Game flow drill)

D 330

Continuous defence - set - attack. Maintenance of game flow; team play between setter and attacker using combination sets (start with shoulder-height passes). Set high if ball is recovered poorly.

"3 on 3" in offensive zone. Begin with overhead pass. Play ball back across the net only after one obligatory pass. Improve different manoeuvres under near-competition conditions.

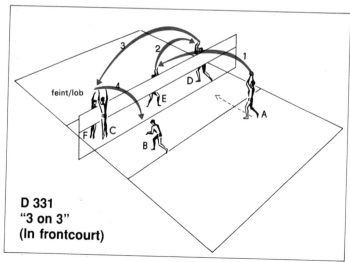

D 331
"3 on 3"
(In frontcourt)

D 331

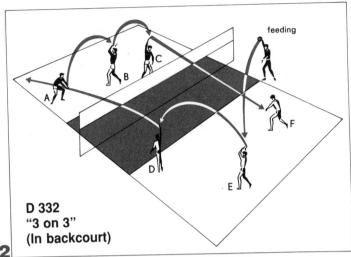

D 332
"3 on 3"
(In backcourt)

D 332

Game style "3 on 3" omitting offensive zones. Attack from backcourt under near-competitive conditions; team co-ordination among defensive players when recovering spikes from backcourt. Throw in new ball if error is made.

"3 on 3" non-stop. Team play between defence - set - offence; active "moving" game and rapid transition to following plays under high physical stress. No tipping to offensive zone; change after five minutes. Controlled game-like drill.

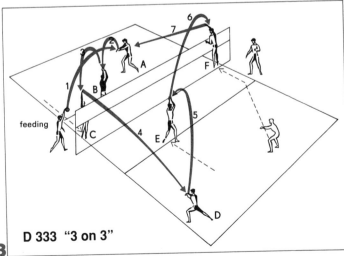

D 333 "3 on 3"

D 333

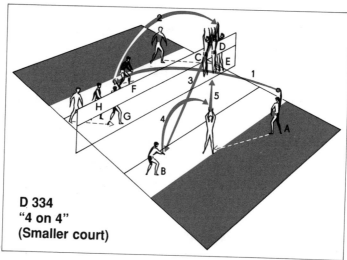

D 334
"4 on 4"
(Smaller court)

D 334

"4 on 4" on smaller court. Emphasis on block attack and coverage as well as defence as frontcourt player not involved in block. Controlled spikes (offspeeds, tips) or hit block offensively or spike to position 4.

"4 on 4" on normal court. Block/defence, preparation and conclusion of counter-attack; throw in ball when an error is committed (to be placed where fault was committed or with other team); no tips into the attack zone.

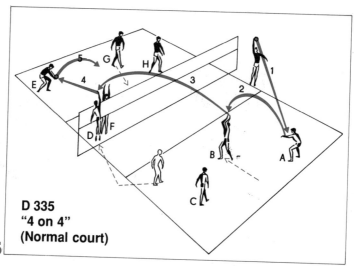

D 335
"4 on 4"
(Normal court)

D 335

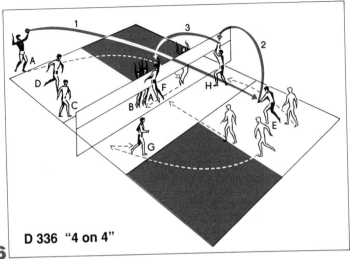

D 336 "4 on 4"

D 336

"4 on 4" omitting specific sections of the court. Serve - three-player line-up receives serve - back-row player sets - attack from positions 3 and 4 against block (no tips to position 2/4) - player G rotates to position 4 after passing serve. Play on half of court, forcing players to play cross-court spikes. Players may attack in any direction provided they hit against the block; attacks mainly from high passes.

Same as Drill 336, using opposite corners of court.

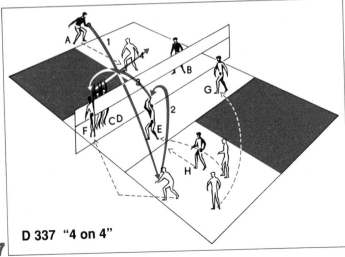

D 337 "4 on 4"

D 337

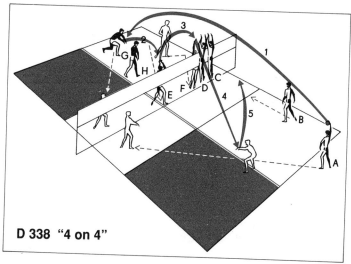

D 338   D 338 "4 on 4"

"4 on 4" omitting specific sections of the court. As in Drills 336 and 337; emphasis is on forcing attack down line or cross-court spike from high passes with two-player block.

"2-on-2" on court set up lengthways. Start with serve or ball thrown in from off court. Move quickly from passing serve/defence to set/attack. Establish good communication on court to determine which player should set.

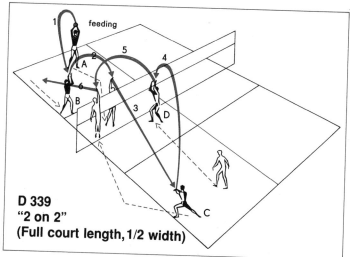

D 339
"2 on 2"
(Full court length, 1/2 width)

D 339

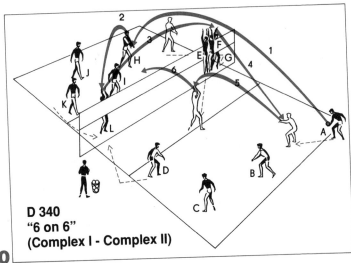

D 340
"6 on 6"
(Complex I - Complex II)

D 340

Complex drilling under near-competitive conditions. One team serves for long period of time (after approximately five minutes position rotation). Variation: if a fault is made, the coach throws in a new ball. The focus is on collective tactics. The game can be made very intense by practising non-stop. Play opens with the serve; the coach then keeps feeding a ball to the team which has completed a play or manoeuvre successfully. Each mistake counts as a point for opponents. This non-stop drill is terminated when a certain number of points is reached.

6 Lead-up Competitive Games for Volleyball

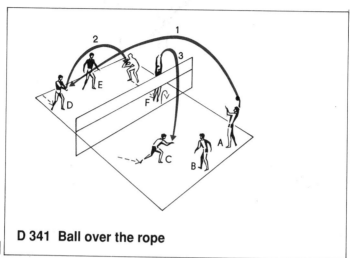

D 341

D 341 Ball over the rope

Ball over the rope.

Ball over the rope helps to prepare for playing volleyball. Two teams play against each other with a ball over a rope (or net). Players try to throw the ball over the net such that it drops onto opponents' court. Opponents try to prevent this by catching the ball and throwing it back.

Teams: 2-4 players.

Net height: 2.5-3 m.

Court: 6 x 12 m (dimensions vary depending upon number of players).

Ball: Any hollow ball or light medicine ball.

Play: The ball may be thrown in any way off court and may be thrown or caught in any fashion.

Scoring: Played against time limit or up to win a certain number of points. Each mistake counts as a point for opponent.

Faults: Ball falls to the floor, ball or players touch net or rope, ball is thrown out. Change after each mistake or after five throws-in.

Rules: Throw the ball from same spot it was caught; must pass once on own side of court; begin by throwing ball from service area; throwing - passing to opponent.

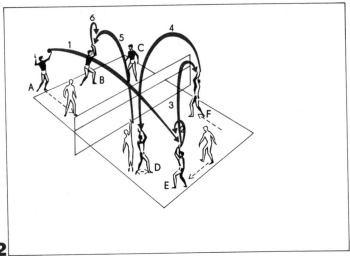

D 342

Ball over the net
With this form, game rules gradually become more similar to those of volleyball, providing important prerequisites (game rules, observing the ball, positional play, watching teammates and opponents, controlling playing area, position in relation to ball, etc.).

Variation 1: Ball over the net and catching it.
     Catch ball with both hands (ten-point position) above forehead, then throw/shoot using set-like motion to partner.
A team must contact the ball three times: (1) play ball up into air - catch - throw or throw and play to partner; (2) catch - play/pass or throw to player; (3) play immediately to opponent, catch - throw or play - pass.
Receiver and second player play directly; third player catches the ball and throws it to opponent.
     Game rules, teams and court (long or narrow, short or wide) may be varied as in ball over the rope. Net height should be varied between 2 and 3 m.

Variation 2: Ball over the net with double play (toss to self, then perform a proper volleyball skill, i.e., catch, toss to self, volley to teammate etc.).
     This playing style is very similar to the "3 on 3" systems. It can be used at this point in the training programme or also as a transitional stage from "4 on 4" to regular volleyball.
     Ball is thrown in (or underarm serve is used). All subsequent plays are made without catching, or throwing (play ball 1-2 times into the air; pass

to partner).

At least one mandatory pass to teammate is required.

Teams: 2-4 players.

Net height: 2.5-3 m.

Court: 3-6 m wide, 3-5 m long or normal volleyball court when there is a larger number of players.

All other specifications are largely the same as those for the types described thus far, but special provisions can always be made. Passing should be evaluated using the standards in volleyball.

Note: In the following types of games volleyball-specific skills are used almost exclusively; however, requirements such as those found in ball over the net can always be used in the teaching progression.

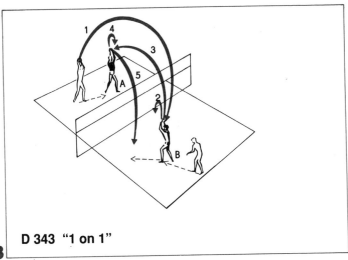

D 343

D 343 "1 on 1"

"1 on 1".
The game "1 on 1" aids in perfecting overhead passing.
Court size: 3x6 m, max. 4x6 m.
Net height: 2.20-2.40 m.

This style can be used with or without an intermediate play (such as play to self first). Two competitive forms are recommended: (1) Pairs of players pass the ball back and forth without interruption; (2) competition according to volleyball rules (players should be allowed to make one or two passes to self).

A variation of the "1 on 1" play is volleyball tennis. For this a long, narrow court (3x6-9 m) is used. Player lets the ball coming from opponent bounce, runs into playing position underneath the ball and plays it back with or without a pass to himself. The following special rule may be incorporated: bounce the ball twice on own court but not twice in a row.

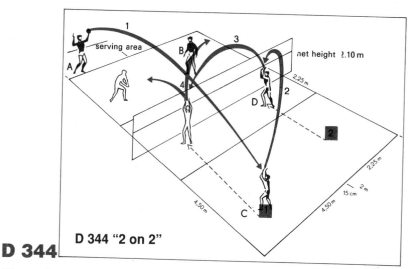

D 344

D 344 "2 on 2"

"2 on 2"

International volleyball rules apply, in principle, for all competitive forms of games. Only the most essential features are described below.

Teams: 2 starting players, 2 substitute players.

Court position: Playing positions 1 and 2. Both players are frontcourt and backcourt players. Immediately following serve players may not rotate on own half of court. This is to prevent players from assuming favourite positions and to prevent early specialization. Over the course of continuous play such changes are possible depending upon the situation.

Scoring: 2 winning sets; a set is finished when a team has scored 10 points.

Specific provisions for faults: All overarm serves, all offensive jump movements, block actions, falling onto one or both knees (except defensive roll), direct pass of serve to opponent.

Technical requirements: Underarm serve, overhead pass (set-up), defensive plays all with overhead pass, standing offensive pass.

Tactical requirements: Gradual compliance with tactical rules, motion towards the ball, positioning for set-up and offensive pass, team play.

When introducing the game, catching and throwing may be allowed. (When receiving serve, play ball up into the air, catch it, then play or throw it to partner; throw ball before set-up.)

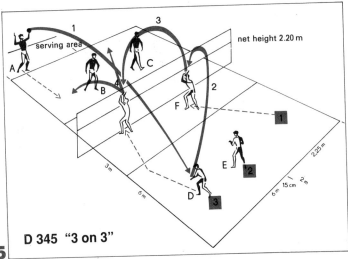

D 345 "3 on 3"

D 345

"3 on 3"

Teams: 3 starting players, 3 substitute players.

Court position: Positions 1, 2 and 3 (see diagram). All players play frontcourt and backcourt. No change in position is allowed immediately after serve has been hit (see Drill 344).

Scoring and specific provisions: Partially as in "2 on 2" (observe new tactical requirements).

Technical requirements: Underarm serve, bump, reception of serve, forward and back set-up, offensive pass, standing off-speed (later while jumping), overarm serve and bump recovery, introduction of falling overhead pass as court pass and pass.

Tactical requirements: Team play on defensive line 1:2 (1 front, 2 back) or 0:3 (all backcourt), targeted serves, direct pass to frontcourt setter or into empty area of court (position 3), decision as to direction of set.

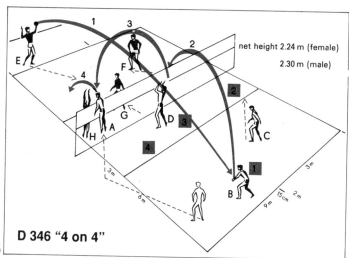

net height 2.24 m (female)
2.30 m (male)

D 346 "4 on 4"

D 346

"4 on 4"

Teams: 4 starting players, 4 substitute players.

Court position: Game positions 1, 2, 3 and 4 (see diagram). Players at positions 2, 3 and 4 are frontcourt players; player at position 1 is backcourt player. No rotation is permitted immediately after serve. Player on court position 1 may not stand in front of player at position 3.

Scoring: 2 winning sets up to 15 points with at least 2 point advantage (16:14 etc.).

Specific provisions for faults: Only frontcourt players may carry out offensive plays in offensive area, falling onto knees (except court defence roll), direct pass of serve to opponent.

Technical requirements: Overarm serve (tennis serve/floating serve), one-man block, standing/jump spike (lob), one- and two-hand tips (from jump); introduce simple offensive combinations if possible.

Tactical requirements: Team play on line 1:3, block coverage, conduct as frontcourt player not involved in blocking, overall team play between block/court defence, otherwise as in "3 on 3" style.

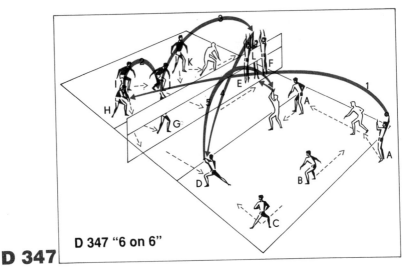

D 347 | D 347 "6 on 6"

"6 on 6" (international match style)

This is the ultimate goal of this training program. The game is now played according to international competitive rules. Every player and the teams themselves must perfect their skills continuously in order to be able to play even better. Although they can derive pleasure from playing at every level of performance, players experience the game in a richer, more lasting way with the increasing mastery of its technical and tactical skills. Chances of victory in competitions increase, and provide an incentive. The more industriously they practise, the more confident players will be of their ability to perform, the more aesthetic pleasure they will gain in the skills mastered and about their success in competition.

7 Sequence Illustrations of Key Game Skills and Their Description

S 1

Underarm serve
- Legs shoulder width apart, left leg forward for right-handed players, trunk bent slightly forwards.
- Trunk twisted slightly when swinging arm back; toss ball arm's length in front of body with one hand.
- Arm stretched when hitting ball, hand cupped tightly together.

Overarm serve with spin (tennis serve)
- Legs apart, left leg forward for right-handed players.
- Toss ball up high with both hands, draw or pull hitting shoulder back.
- Hit the ball with arm stretched and cupped hand. Follow through with active use of wrist to produce topspin.

S 2

S 3

Overarm serve without spin (floating serve)

- Legs apart, hold ball to left approximately at head height, hitting arm up, hitting shoulder back.
- Hitting hand straight, wrists taut and flexed (back of hands - forearm – one line).
- Toss ball up not too high, without spin, in front of hitting shoulder.
- Hit ball hard at centre, do not follow through.

Lateral floating serve ("Japanese hook")

- Straddle position sideways to net; toss ball low without spin (hit almost out of hand).
- Arm swing variable, ball hit at mid-point (hand flexed, with edge of thumb), arm stretched and locked.
- Hitting arm and trunk should move slowly when hitting; do not swing through (ensures quicker, shorter, cleaner shot).

S 4

S 5

Lateral overhead serve with spin (hook serve)
- Straddle position laterally to net; throw ball with one or both hands above head.
- Bend to the right when swinging arm back; hitting arm stretched out swings farther behind body; do not bend at hips.
- Hitting motion by means of stretching legs and trunk; push hitting shoulder forward and up; use circular movement of arms (stretched) and hit ball above head.
- Hand cupped and taut, bent at wrist.
- When hitting turn shoulder axis towards direction of shot.
- Swing hitting arm completely through; turn (jump) around onto other foot.

Passing serve in front of body
- Ready position: legs slightly apart or straddled, move on the spot, arms relaxed at side of body.
- Body pointing to play direction, firm stance.
- Arms stretched, forearms flexed, thumbs pointing downwards, hands fixed, ball contact on first third of forearm.
- Playing ball using legs, shoulder and minimum use of arms.

S 6

S 7

Passing serve from side of body
- Ready position: legs apart or straddled, one foot leading, movement on spot.
- Foot of the receiving side set back, shoulder axis almost parallel with trajectory of ball.
- Lift shoulder of striking arm (tilt arms), let the approaching ball hit you.
- Arms move slightly up in direction of play, leg of ball receiving side is comfortably extended.

Passing serve (low balls served tight to net)

S 8

S 9

Sidearm passing of serve

Overhead pass
- Quick movement to playing position with normal use of arms.
- Turn to face direction of play, firm straddle position, one foot leading,
- head - ball - target in one line.
  Bend arms, legs during approach of ball.
- Hands cupped, flex fingers and wrist activity.
- Play ball at approximately forehead level; legs, body, arms and wrists fully stretched.

S 10

S 11

Back overhead pass
- Quick movement to playing position with normal use of arms.
- Square back to direction of designed pass, firm straddle position, one foot leading.
- Bend arms, legs during approach of ball.
- Remain erect when playing ball; only pull the head back; play above the head; when stretching the entire body push hip slightly forward.

Lateral falling overhead pass
- Quick movement to playing position; wide step and drop body behind and underneath ball while facing play; pivot about foot which took wide step.
- Ball played (in front of face, above head) by stretching arms; cupped hand formation, flex fingers and wrist activity.
- Player rolls onto buttocks to land on his back.

S 12

S 13

Overhead pass with backwards roll
- Run quickly underneath ball facing play, dropping down (legs apart to straddle position).
- Play ball approximately at forehead only with arms stretched.
- Pass first, then roll onto buttocks and back.

Overhead jump pass/offensive pass
- Assume approach position quickly.
- Long step with the right leg, left leg turned slightly inward and set down in front of right leg; take off with both legs and active use of arms.
- Play the ball at highest point in take-off above head by stretching arms or using wrists.
- Soft, two-legged landing.

S 14

S 15

One-handed tip from jump
● Move up towards the ball, swing back of arm and land as in spike.
● Break off hitting movement early and "push" ball beside or over block with arm almost completely extended; use wrists actively to lift the ball over the block.
● Soft, two-legged landing.

Spike in direction of approach (normal attack)
● Assume approach position quickly (diagonally to net).
● Long step with the right leg, left leg turned inward and set down in front of right leg; heels touch ground first.
● Hitting shoulder is pulled back, explosive two-legged take-off with active use of arms swinging forwards and upwards.
● Hitting shoulder farther back when swinging (bring shoulder axis forward).
● With arm extended hit ball in front of body at highest point of take-off.
● Cup hand around ball, bring shoulder forward, and swing hitting arm completely through.

S 16

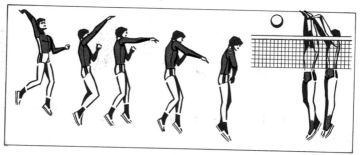

S 17

Spike across the body

Advanced players do not use the same offensive style for approach and hitting direction. As opposed to the twist shot, hitting arm moves in direction of spike (across body), shoulder axis hardly changes from its angle approach direction.

S 18

Lateral spike (hook)
- Approach and take off as in spike in run-up direction, but at acute angle to net.
- During take-off left arm swings up in front of body, right arm drops (hand on thigh).
- Circular hitting movement of stretched right arm; delayed turning of hitting shoulder and trunk in direction of shot.
- During hit hand closed, flexed, bent at wrist in direction of spike (hand from above diagonally around ball).
- Left arm locked in front of body during hit, two-legged soft landing.

S 19

Spike with turn
- Approach, take-off, swinging of arm same as spike in approach direction (normal, straight-ahead attack).
- More acute approach angle, take-off position farther to the right (run around ball slightly).
- Jump first, then turn in mid-air and hit.
- Body continues to turn after shot; trunk used more than normal because of turn.
- Forward landing or with right shoulder towards net (shoulder axis changed in relation to take-off position).

S 20

One-man block
- Ready starting position.
- Quick movement to block position (shuffle with feet short distance, run and use arms over greater distance using cross step); square to net.
- Take-off from slightly crouched position and arms from shoulder level.
- Bring arms and hands over the net to meet the ball until they are stretched, shoulders remain behind arms (do not push head through arms).
- Hands are pushed strongly down from the wrist to force the ball into the opponents' court.
- After contact bring arms back, soft landing.

Two-handed bump in front of body
- Straddle position on balls of feet, one foot leading, movement on the spot.
- Bump ball close to the floor, arms stretched and parallel in front of body, shoulder joints locked, shoulders pushed forward.
- Do not stretch body when contacting ball; flex at the knees; let ball bounce off arms; straighten up after recovery.

S 21

S 22

Two-player block

- Ready position close to net; place feet on ground or run quickly to block position (see single-player block).
- Arms bent during take-off and brought slightly in front of body; take off such that block is closed above the net; jump vertically close to each other.
- All four hands form a defensive shield; fingers spread slightly, hands rigid.
- Reach far over net; cup hands over ball and push down forcefully.
- Pull arms back quickly; land ready for play.

S 23

One-handed lateral recovery, with slide
- Straddle position on balls of feet, one foot leading, movement on the spot.
- Quick run to playing position, wide drop step.
- Pivot heels outward, square body to direction of play, stretch body and push body flat underneath ball.
- Recover ball close to floor to side of body (with forearm, fist, tightly closed hand).
- Smooth landing on thigh, buttocks, and back.

One-handed recovery forward (dive)
- Ready position as in other defensive styles.
- Run forward quickly, crouch down and bend trunk forward.
- Take off powerfully with leg closest to ball, dive flat and forward; stretch both arms forward.
- Play ball with back of hand (also with fist) of the extended arm.
- Smooth landing on chest, stomach, thigh; both hands are placed on the floor one after the other, lessening impact.

S 24

S 25

Recovery with roll (one-handed, two-handed)
- Same as in lateral recovery up to and including turn in direction of play.
- Two- or one-handed recovery laterally or in front of body.
- Roll sideways onto back and buttocks (with the ball far in front of body; recovery similar to forward dive; very quick rotation around longitudinal axis of body; roll over (remain stretched).

S 26

Two-handed bump in front of body